Leadership, According to Solomon

Alannah,

You are a role
model — a total
example of wise
leadership + character
Always, Jan Halles

Leadership, According to Solomon

A Story of One School Leader's Quest for Wisdom

Jan Irons Harris

Foreword by Professor Yong Zhao

Published in partnership with the
American Association of School Administrators

ROWMAN & LITTLEFIELD
Lanham • Boulder • New York • London

All proceeds from this book will go to Childhaven Children's Home, Cullman, Alabama, United States.

"Religion that God our Father accepts as pure and faultless is this: to look after orphans and widows in their distress. . . ." (James 1:27).

Scripture taken from the HOLY BIBLE, NEW INTERNATIONAL VERSION. Copyright 1973, 1978, 1984. International Bible Society unless otherwise noted. Used by permission of Zondervan. All rights reserved.

The "NIV" and "New International Version" trademarks are registered in the United States Patent and Trademark Office by International Bible Society. Use of either trademark requires the permission of International Bible Society.

Published in partnership with the American Association of School Administrators

Published by Rowman & Littlefield
A wholly owned subsidiary of
The Rowman & Littlefield Publishing Group, Inc.
4501 Forbes Boulevard, Suite 200, Lanham, Maryland 20706
www.rowman.com

Unit A, Whitacre Mews, 26-34 Stannary Street, London SE11 4AB, United Kingdom

British Library Cataloguing in Publication Information Available

Library of Congress Cataloging-in-Publication Data

Includes bibliographic references.
978-1-4758-3010-1 (cloth : alk. paper)
978-1-4758-3011-8 (pbk. : alk. paper)
978-1-4758-3012-5 (Electronic)

♾ ™ The paper used in this publication meets the minimum requirements of American National Standard for Information Sciences Permanence of Paper for Printed Library Materials, ANSI/NISO Z39.48-1992.

Printed in the United States of America

Dedicated to my favorite teachers:
Carolyn Eck, teacher of mathematics
Wayne Higgins, 6th grade teacher
Brenda Mitchell, home economics teacher

Contents

Foreword

The world today is in desperate need of wise leaders, not only in education, but also in other professions, especially in politics. The massive societal challenges have put many wicked and foolish people in important offices around the world recently and they are threatening the future of humanity. These people are entrusted with great power but they exemplify just the opposite of King Solomon's qualities of wisdom: vision, knowledge, ethics, humility, self-control, counsel, and understanding.

They have no vision, or worse, a vision for a divided world, pitching people against each other. They refuse to seek knowledge, or they reject facts and truth as alternative facts or fake news. They ignore ethics and seek injustice and discrimination against people who are different from them. They view humility as a sign of weakness and seek credit for accomplishments they have not contributed to.

They have little self-control and lash out on social media, without any consideration of possible consequences. They do not seek counsel from advisors and instead refute differing suggestions as attacks. They do not understand their fellow citizens; instead they are quick to quarrel, to brag, to start unnecessary battles, and to spread gossip.

These political leaders should study Solomon's proverbs, like Katy and Dr. Martin, the two educators whose journey to seek wisdom is told by Dr. Harris in this book. While the book is about educational leadership, the moral of the stories can benefit all who seek to be wise, instead of foolish and wicked, leaders in any profession.

More important, education is about cultivating wise leaders. I see the ascendance of foolish and wicked people into high offices as a failure of education in this regard. A successful education cannot be measured by test scores, but by the growth of wisdom. A wise education leader is one who curates an environment that fosters wisdom in all students. Dr. Harris's book is also an example of a good education.

We draw our inspirations from different sources. Apparent cultural differences should not artificially prevent us from learning from each other. Growing up in China, I was not aware of the Bible or Solomon. Yet Solomon's qualities of a wise leader resonate with me the same way teachings of great Chinese philosophers such as Confucius do. At a time when technology brings human beings into ever-closer contact with each other, it is forever more important for us to learn from each other and "understand" each other, as Solomon would do.

Yong Zhao, PhD
Foundation Distinguished Professor, University of Kansas

Preface

Recently, I read an article on how to "live a long life." The article offered the typical longevity advice on eating, exercise, and stress. But it occurred to me that this article, like so many others, did not really help the reader learn how to "live," but rather how to survive. Though its admonitions regarding health and nutrition may have been quality, there is so much more involved in truly living.

In contrast, Dr. Jan Irons Harris understands that physical survival is only one part of the greater equation that leads to living a long and prosperous life, and indeed, enjoying a long and prosperous career, too. Through her stories and admonitions, which rely on real-life experiences and the timeless wisdom of Solomon, she is able to offer refreshing encouragement to school administrators who often feel overwhelmed by the weight of their daily burdens.

Indeed, school administrators are tireless advocates for children and often work fifty to sixty hours a week and more. They handle security, discipline, finances, building services, meal service, athletics and extracurricular events, not to mention making sure children under their care have the resources and opportunities for optimal learning. And yet, like our story's heroine, Dr. Katy Carter, most enter this field because they experience a deep sense of calling and mission. Unfortunately, that calling and mission can later get lost in the fray of daily work.

Dr. Harris reminds us that inner purpose is, indeed, the most important aspect of an effective school administrator. As readers weave through this beautiful parable, they are reminded again of their deepest sense of calling, the wonder of learning from one another, the joy of sharing life's highs and lows with colleagues and friends, and the timeless virtues expressed by Solomon in Proverbs. Other books and articles will assist you in lowering your cholesterol and "surviving," but *Leadership, According to Solomon* will cheer your soul and lift you up to live life to its fullest.

Dr. Eric Mackey
Executive Director
School Superintendents of Alabama

Acknowledgments

Writing this book would not be possible without the following individuals. Heartfelt thanks to . . .

Publisher Tom Koerner and Rowman & Littlefield for the opportunity to publish this book, and to Tom and editor Carlie Wall for their guidance and oversight.

Dr. Jimmy Minichello and the American Association of School Administrators for copublishing *Leadership, According to Solomon.*

My parents, Bobby and Sarah Irons, and my sister, Rhonda Anderton, along with my family and friends, for their encouragement and support.

My colleagues who contributed to *Leadership, According to Solomon.*

My husband, Dennis Wholey Harris, for his infinite love, enduring friendship, and incredible support editing my book and making sacrifices so it could be written, and most importantly, I thank God, the giver of all blessings, for the opportunity to write this book to support my current and future colleagues as well as the good work at Childhaven Children's Home in Cullman, Alabama.

Introduction

Wisdom > Silver + Gold + Rubies

This book unites my two passions—education and bible literacy. *Leadership, According to Solomon* is not a traditional textbook. It's a story about one school leader's quest for wisdom. It's a story that delineates seven qualities, according to Solomon, that successful, wise leaders possess. It's a story that reflects my imagination of perfect beginnings and endings. The characters in this story represent the best of us—who we are and who we long to be in our oscillating leadership roles.

Katy Carter, a master teacher and principal, aspires to become a superintendent. She remembers a favorite graduate school professor who extolled the merits of identifying and securing a mentor. So Katy asks her superintendent, Dr. Martin, to serve as her mentor, and he agrees. Through lessons provided by her mentor, Katy learns the true meaning of leadership.

Dr. Martin defines a job description for leaders, and identifies a leader for Katy to study: King Solomon, the richest, wisest king that ever lived. He introduces Katy to Solomon's book of Proverbs, found in the Bible. These timeless truths from America's favorite book equip Katy, a successful school administrator, to become a better leader. Dr. Martin shares, from his observations and from studying Solomon's proverbs, seven qualities that wise leaders possess:

1. Wise Leaders Are Visionary
2. Wise Leaders Are Seekers of Knowledge
3. Wise Leaders Are Ethical
4. Wise Leaders Are Humble
5. Wise Leaders Are Self-Controlled

6. Wise Leaders Seek Counsel
7. Wise Leaders Understand Others

Additionally, Katy and her mentor provide examples of leaders who person-
ify each of the seven qualities. Throughout the book, Katy reflects upon the
proverbs related to each of the seven qualities. In the conclusion, Dr. Martin
talks about the three types of people: the foolish, the wicked, and the wise.
The reader will find a compilation of proverbs related to each of the seven
qualities in the appendix, along with reflective questions for each section of
the book.

Like Solomon, Katy is not perfect; she wants to grow into a mature and
wise leader as she assumes more responsibility and seeks continual improvement through professional learning and reflection on experiences. Over time,
and with guidance from her trusted mentor, she develops a clearer understanding of what is required to improve her skillset and become an enduring,
wise, and even more successful leader.

It is my hope that you and I will be wise leaders. May we embrace lessons
from this story that will be helpful to us as we, like Solomon, strive to solve
problems with wisdom, and, therefore, help others entrusted to our care.
Solomon said, "Blessed are those who find wisdom . . . for she is more
profitable than silver and yields better returns than gold. She is more precious
than rubies; nothing you desire can compare with her" (Proverbs 3:13–15).

Prologue

Kathleen Estelle Olive was destined to become a teacher. Family members and friends all said so. Even though Kathleen was her first name, everybody called Kathleen "Katy" or "Miss Katy Elle" when she pretended to be a teacher.

Named after her grandmothers, Katy Elle reflected characteristics from both matriarchs. Her daddy's mother, Kathleen, was a beloved elementary school principal whose portrait reverently hung in the lobby of the school, where she served as leader for thirty-two years. When young Katy Elle declared that "playing school" was her favorite activity, family members said she was just like Nana Olive. Katy looked like Granny Estelle and mirrored her kind disposition and stellar work ethic. Granny Estelle worked in the cafeteria of the school where Nana Olive served as principal.

Sharpened pencils and colorful crayons invited all who visited Katy's bedroom to capture new ideas on clean paper. Katy's artistic creations adorned the kitchen's refrigerator door. Books were filed in alphabetical order in her bookcase. Expectant energy filled Katy Elle's bedroom— like all places of learning.

When Miss Katy Elle played "school," her student roster included the names of dolls, neighborhood friends, and family members. Mother revealed herself to be a hard worker and a seeker of knowledge. She became an "A" student. Miss Katy Elle exhibited a positive demeanor as she taught her students. She smiled, as teachers do, and spoke with a Southern lilt while reading, lecturing, and posing thought-provoking questions.

Miss Katy Elle's students were all gifted, just in different areas. Some students were gifted singers, like Gena, while others were better athletes or scholars or artists. They craved outdoor physical activities and creative opportunities for music and art. They longed for special events such as the favorite tea party on Grandmother's quilt or the celebratory parade. Her students often created and performed plays, and sang songs on Katy Elle's clean carport.

Katy Elle excelled as a student, as she truly loved real school. Teachers could depend on her to raise her hand quickly to demonstrate her preparation and eagerness to answer questions and learn. Katy Elle's elementary school teacher noticed she had a proclivity for mathematics, and invited her to become a tutor for students who struggled in the subject. This experience solidified the fact that Miss Katy Elle would become a teacher, and she happily embraced this truth.

Yes, Miss Katy Elle was destined to become a teacher because she was given a gift—the ability to teach—and she knew it. She recognized the truth that some people have the ability to understand and explain a concept to seekers of knowledge, while others do not have the patience for it.

At Katy's ten-year high school reunion, her English teacher returned essays entitled "Ten Years from Now" to graduates who attended. Katy Elle shared with her husband her treasured essay that revealed her desire to become a teacher. Daniel Patrick Carter was her college sweetheart, best friend, and now spouse. Katy Elle took a moment to reflect. She was indeed a teacher, and was also in graduate school and happily married.

Katy Elle loved school. Her "J-O-B" was never a job. Her work made her heart joyfully sing when she was successful in helping her students learn. Sure, there were a few trying times, but she was content—even peaceful—in her choice to become a teacher. Katy knew she was making a positive difference in the lives of her students.

Katy loved bells and the structure school provided. Mostly, she loved the energy and excitement of working with young people. She loved the newness of it all—having a new class of students each year to teach, and continually improving her teaching.

Ms. Carter, as Katy was called by her students, displayed high expectations for all of her students to learn, regardless of their giftedness. Through her glasses, she saw that all students were lovable and deserving of her time, attention, and teaching. She was a competent, caring teacher who provided academic rigor in her classroom. Furthermore, Ms. Carter was a role model due to being self-disciplined and successful in her personal life.

Ms. Carter, a gracious teacher who chose to believe the best about her students and the people with whom she worked, was strict. She was not one to be taken advantage of, but she was steadfast in her willingness to distribute a second chance. Needless to say, Ms. Carter's love for her students was returned to her. She was a respected master teacher. Because of Katy's success in the classroom, she became an assistant principal at the urging of her principal. Later, the opportunity to become a principal became hers.

Katy found serving as principal more challenging in that she was responsible for an entire school, but it was rewarding and it aligned with her gift of teaching. She continued to learn by pursuing her doctorate in school administration during this time. Principal Carter enjoyed working with teachers and support staff, and she loved her students. She reached out to parents and students when there was a need. Ms. Carter was there for her students, staff, and parents, and they knew it.

After several years of serving successfully as high school principal, and after earning her doctorate, Katy's supervisor told her that she should consider becoming a superintendent. So, after she talked to those within her circle of influence about the matter, Dr. Carter determined that she wished to become a superintendent in order to influence the lives of students in an entire school district in a positive manner. She needed a plan. How would she proceed?

THE LESSON ON MENTORING

Katy recalled an especially meaningful class she had while completing her graduate work. She told Daniel after supper one Sunday night that her professor encouraged the graduate students to seek mentors for guidance throughout their professional and personal life. Dr. Searby had said that leaders learn from different sources, but they learn the most when they learn from wise and experienced individuals who mentor them.

Daniel selected classical music for them to listen to while Katy filled her red teakettle with water and placed it on the lit gas stove to boil. She opened her laptop to search for her notes from this class. The whistle of the teakettle prompted Katy to return to the stove. She prepared two cups of medicinal green tea with local honey and fresh squeezed lemon juice.

Katy began to read her lecture notes and an article from Dr. Linda Searby, which included her own testimony of how mentoring helped her in her life. She could almost hear her professor's friendly, calming voice as she read to herself:

> The concept of mentoring is a universally recognized, socially enacted practice that has its roots in ancient Greek culture.
>
> In Homer's *Odyssey*, Mentor was actually the goddess Athena, embodied as a male who came to earth to be entrusted with the watch-care and guidance of Telemachus, the son of Odysseus, when Odysseus went off to fight the Trojan War. From this myth developed the word *mentor* and the concept of *mentoring*, traditionally defined as a relationship between an older, more experienced person and a younger, less experienced protégé for the purpose of developing the protégé, personally and professionally.
>
> As an area of research, mentoring is relatively "young." Foundational studies in mentoring, which resulted in books, were conducted by Daniel Le-

vinson in 1978 (*The Seasons of a Man's Life*) and Kathy Kram in 1985 (*Mentoring at Work: Developmental Relationships in Organizational Life*). Since then, researchers examined the predictors, processes, and outcomes of mentoring, the role and influence of personality, race, gender, and culture on the relationships, and how mentoring influences the development of leadership and career trajectories.

Global economic changes have impacted all cultures, and increased diversity in the workforce in all professions has altered individuals' career relationships. Because of this, formal mentoring programs are being developed in almost every profession (Ehrich, Hansford, and Tennent 2004). Mentoring has been found to assist with professional socialization, which is defined as "learning about the broader set of expectations, skills, behaviors, and performance demands associated with a particular profession" (Lankau and Scandura 2007, 97).

According to Ragins and Kram (2007), "At its best, mentoring can be a life-altering relationship that inspires mutual growth, learning, and development. Its effects can be remarkable, profound, and enduring; mentoring relationships have the capacity to transform individuals, groups, organizations, and communities" (p. 3). Another primary reason that organizations are developing mentoring programs is to retain talented individuals who have exemplified leadership potential (Ramaswami and Dreher 2010).

As Katy continued reading her notes, it was like being back in class listening to Dr. Searby lecture: "Mentoring, as an area of research and scholarship, is a relatively young field, but recent research confirms that when individuals are able to choose their own mentors and create their own goals for the mentoring relationship, their satisfaction in the mentoring relationship is high." Katy recalled Dr. Searby sharing that the mentoring relationships she experienced contributed significantly to her development as a leader, and helped her to develop resilience in times of professional challenges.

Dr. Searby told her students about her first "formal" mentoring relationship. She was an elementary school principal, and felt a tug to think about a different administrative role. She knew she needed guidance in thinking about a transition, and how to go about networking for such a move. She knew she wanted a mentor with whom she could discuss these matters, and she also knew whom she wanted to ask. But it took Dr. Searby almost a year to gather the courage to ask her superintendent to mentor her, and, when asked, she quickly agreed.

Dr. Searby treasured those times when she could glean her insights and wise advice. Dr. Searby shared that her colleagues who had been assigned mentors often felt their mentors did not have much of an interest in helping them to succeed. The mentors she chose for herself were difference-makers in her life because they believed in her, encouraged her, calmed her self-doubts, and affirmed her strengths. They helped her to achieve more than she thought was possible. Now she sought to "pay it forward" by mentoring emerging leaders as well.

Katy told Daniel, "Dr. Searby said mentors are needed at every stage of life because people are usually not very good at being objective about their strengths, or 'growing edges.' She said a mentor can hold up a mirror for individuals to see themselves more clearly, and also help make both personal and career transitions. Furthermore, she said it is not a sign of weakness to seek a mentor; it is a sign of strength."

Daniel replied, "The paradigm of mentoring has changed. The old paradigm was that one needs a mentor because of *deficiencies* in performance in the workplace. But it's cool to have a mentor now. In fact, it's almost a status symbol to have a mentor. Young professionals are seeking out experienced individuals whom they admire and are approaching them about participating in a regular mentoring relationship."

Katy confided that she wanted to have a mentor. She said, "Dr. Ronnie Martin would be an excellent mentor." Daniel nodded his head in agreement.

Katy made the decision, like Dr. Searby, to move forward in her quest to seek out a mentor. The next morning she made an appointment to speak with her superintendent, Dr. Ronnie Martin.

KATY'S MENTOR

Katy was appreciative of the superintendent's willingness to meet with her the next week. She had never been to the superintendent's office to talk about her personal career goals. It was a bit intimidating, she thought, as she sat in the waiting area's wooden chair prior to their meeting. Dr. Searby's story of how she sought out her mentor echoed in Katy's mind and served as a source of strength at that moment.

Because Katy admired and respected her superintendent, she valued any advice he would kindly offer. Just as her mind was drifting to the questions she intended to propose that day, Dr. Martin appeared before her and said, "Hello, Dr. Carter. Welcome to the superintendent's office. Come in." As they walked into his office and toward the conference table, she noticed that the door to the superintendent's office had a window in it with the school system logo etched in the glass.

Katy told Dr. Martin that she admired and respected his work and the way he lived his life. She reminded him that during her tenure with the school district, she had successfully served as a teacher, assistant principal, and principal. Katy told Dr. Martin she recently completed her doctorate in school administration, and was ready to focus on the next chapter of her career—possibly pursuing the superintendency. She asked Dr. Martin if he saw her as a potential superintendent candidate, and if so, would he serve as her mentor.

Katy nervously waited for Dr. Martin's response, wondering if he could hear her heart beating at a pace two or three times the normal rate. It began to feel rather warm in his friendly office. She felt exposed. It took courage for her to sit before him now.

After what seemed to be an eternity, but in actuality was only an effective teacher's pause, Dr. Martin told Katy he believed she was a fine candidate for the superintendent position. Katy's exemplary record demonstrated her leadership ability, work ethic, passion for education, and professionalism. In each position she managed the level of responsibility given to her well. Most importantly, Katy demonstrated through her actions that she truly cared about those entrusted to her supervision. Dr. Martin agreed to serve as Katy's mentor and stated it was an honor to be asked to do so.

Katy took a deep breath, smiled and replied, "Thank you, Dr. Martin." He explained that he liked to mentor others because he was the beneficiary of others who mentored him. In return for his willingness to mentor Katy, he expected her to do the following:

1. Mentor someone coming behind Katy,
2. allow Dr. Martin to kindly share the truth with her, and
3. commit to the learning assignments he planned to give her.

Katy not only liked his insightful expectations, she was inspired by them. She quickly affirmed his expectations. She was willing to mentor others coming behind her, and complete any assignments he gave her. Katy didn't understand what Dr. Martin meant when he said he wanted to share the truth with her. Dr. Martin explained, "Most people have politically correct relationships. And, as such, they walk around in partial darkness when those around them have the ability to illuminate not only circumstances, but strengths and weaknesses as well."

In truth, Katy's work history was outstanding, and Dr. Martin was pleased with her expressed desire to become a superintendent of education. During their conversation, he explained that he desired to be a wise leader, and live his personal life wisely. Therefore, he sought wisdom and accountability through his mentors. Through the years Dr. Martin developed a list of qualities that successful, wise leaders seem to possess.

Katy reached for her black journal. In gold ink, letters penned in calligraphy united to spell her full name, Kathleen Estelle Olive Carter—centered and properly facing downward on its spine. She opened her black journal and began to write on the page with a black felt tip pen. Dr. Martin noted her attention to detail as he explained that, through his personal studies and observations, he had found that there are seven qualities that wise leaders seem to have in their personal and professional lives:

1. Wise leaders are visionary
2. Wise leaders are seekers of knowledge
3. Wise leaders are ethical
4. Wise leaders are humble
5. Wise leaders are self-controlled
6. Wise leaders seek counsel
7. Wise leaders understand others

Dr. Martin identified these qualities from Solomon's book on wise living, the book of Proverbs, in the Best-Selling Book of All Time, the Bible. He liked to read one of the thirty-one chapters each day. Dr. Martin defined this list of practical truths about life and leadership as he reflected on his own practices and observations of successful leaders. This list continued to guide him in his quest for wise leading and living.

Dr. Martin said, "Look at the sixth quality, Katy. Wise leaders seek counsel. See, you are already revealing yourself to be a wise leader. You're here today seeking counsel by asking me to serve as your mentor."

"Thank you, Dr. Martin," Katy said.

Dr. Martin glanced at his watch, looked at his calendar, and said, "Let's meet at this same time next week, if this time is agreeable with your schedule. Until then, your assignment is to read Proverbs—one chapter each day. Keep a journal to take notes about proverbs that relate to your situation. Write these proverbs down along with the chapter and verse from which they came."

Dr. Martin told Katy he would provide the job description for a superintendent—or for any leader—at their next meeting. Also, they would talk about Solomon and start exploring the seven qualities that wise leaders possess. Katy looked at her calendar to confirm their next meeting date and thanked Dr. Martin for his time.

After Katy told Daniel about her meeting with Dr. Martin, they decided they would both make it a priority to read and discuss the book of Proverbs as time allowed. They enjoyed lively conversations about philosophy, religion, and politics. They agreed to set their alarm fifteen minutes earlier each day so they could make time to read the book of Proverbs, one chapter each day, according to the day of the month—like Dr. Martin.

Solomon, the Wise King

A Leader Who Solved Problems

Katy was an early riser, and she liked to go to bed early in order to get a good night's rest. A collector of quotes, she liked Benjamin Franklin's admonition from his 1735 book, *Poor Richard's Almanac*: "Early to bed, early to rise, makes a man healthy, wealthy and wise." She often used Franklin's quote when talking to her students to create an awareness of the importance of sleep.

The morning's early hours are golden, Katy thought, as she poured her first cup of coffee in an inspiring white coffee mug that revealed a friendly, yellow interior upon sipping. As she added cream to her coffee, she gazed upon the front of the mug, where a simple smiley face looked at her. Beneath it, the word "Happy" caught her attention. Happiness was a choice, Katy believed. And Katy chose to be happy. She chose to believe the best in difficult situations, and she chose to believe the best of others.

Before the sun rises, the world is quiet in its darkness, Katy thought as she walked to the kitchen table with the hot coffee warming the cup and her hands simultaneously. She could accomplish twice as much in the early morning hours as she could during the noisy, bustling busyness of the school day. And so it was that Katy was wide awake at 5:00 a.m., sitting at her kitchen's heart pine farm table with her hair uncombed and rumpled, wearing her pajamas and pink chenille robe and her brown, comfy, fur-lined moccasins.

She opened her journal and found the page with her mentor's notes and the seven qualities of wise leaders. She read them aloud slowly as she reflected on each important quality of wise leaders:

1. Visionary

    2. Seekers of knowledge
    3. Ethical
    4. Humble
    5. Self-controlled
    6. Seek counsel
    7. Understand others

When she finished reading the seven qualities, she wrote in her journal:

Objective: To be a successful, wise leader, this aspiring superintendent desires to be visionary, a seeker of knowledge, ethical, humble, and self-controlled. This administrator will seek counsel and strive to understand others.

Then Katy read chapter 8 of Proverbs (because it was the eighth day of the month), highlighting in yellow the verses that seemed to fit her circumstances. She wrote quick notes about the proverbs in her journal with a royal blue calligraphy pen. Katy copied Solomon's advice from verses 10 and 11:

Choose my instruction instead of silver, knowledge rather than choice gold, for wisdom is more precious than rubies, and nothing you desire can compare with her.

Because she loved mathematics, Katy transposed the proverb into a wise equation and wrote it beneath Solomon's words:

Wisdom > Silver + Gold + Rubies

The morning's quiet time ticked away as the sun made its arrival. Katy prepared oatmeal for breakfast—one of their favorite healthy choices to start the day. Daniel joined her in the kitchen as she added walnuts, raisins, flaxseed, and local honey to the hot, steel-cut oatmeal. She served their hot breakfast in simple white bowls. Katy gave one of the bowls to the man who strengthened and encouraged her. He made her life better each day.

As they ate, they discussed the eighth chapter of Proverbs, which Daniel had also read earlier that morning. They talked about wisdom—an invisible quality that permeates the words and actions of the successful leader. And then it was time to get dressed and leave for work and school.

DR. MARTIN PROVIDES A
JOB DESCRIPTION FOR LEADERS

Katy looked forward to meeting with Dr. Martin again. As she read from the book of Proverbs, it seemed odd that a gap existed in her personal journey of learning. She asked herself how it was that she missed Solomon's wise advice during her education. During her childhood, Katy read parts of the Bible, but she did not remember reading the proverbs. Some of the proverbs didn't relate to her situation, but others were amazingly right on target, as if these proverbs were specifically penned with her in mind.

Katy read and reread the proverbs that she had carefully and beautifully transferred to her journal. She and Daniel enjoyed talking about the proverbs that applied to each of them and were pleased when they selected and claimed the same verses as favorites.

Katy smiled and greeted Beth, the superintendent's secretary, as she entered the office of the superintendent, five minutes early for her appointment. She was anxious to hear Dr. Martin's job description for a superintendent even though she already knew it. She reviewed the job description posted in the board policy manual in preparation for this meeting. And, having served as a school principal for a number of years, she was aware of the daily responsibilities of the school's chief leader.

Dr. Martin arrived at precisely 4:00 p.m. and welcomed Katy to his office by saying, "It's nice to see you, Dr. Carter. Was it a great day at Independence High School today?"

Katy smiled and replied, "Yes, sir. Every day is a great day at Independence High." She was uplifted because of the consistent optimism and energy displayed by Dr. Martin, a kind and professional gentleman. Even at 4:00 p.m., he was friendly and focused.

Dr. Martin said, "Have you been reading Solomon's Proverbs?"

Katy replied, "Yes, and it continues to be an eye-opening experience learning from the wise king."

Dr. Martin replied, "Wonderful! Keep reading. Now, let's talk about the expectations for any superintendent. What do you think the number one job of a superintendent is, Katy?"

Katy thought about this, remembering the job description she studied, and replied, "School safety. That's the most important task of any school leader. And after school safety, the most important responsibility for the school leader is to improve student achievement. Superintendents are supposed to make sure that students learn and perform well on academic measures."

Dr. Martin replied, "That's true, but the one holistic job description that covers all expectations for a superintendent, or any leader, can be summed up in one sentence: Leaders are expected to solve problems. That's right. Leaders solve problems. Everyday." Katy wrote in her black journal:

Job Description for Leaders: Solve problems.

Dr. Martin continued, "The Master Teacher, Jesus, said, 'In this world you will have trouble.' There are plenty of problems surrounding us. Globally, conflicts or wars and the close proximity of potential wars, terrorism, earthquakes, fires, other natural disasters, hunger, and sickness can be seen. In America, struggles with civil rights can be observed even today, as we sadly still see acts of racism and hatred in American society. Challenges exist with equality, education, immigration, and citizens lament the economy as our elected and appointed leaders strive to create a balanced budget.

"Americans long for low unemployment rates coupled with the dream of 100 percent of students graduating ready for college or career, or possibly joining the military. The list of problems is never-ending. But, there is a shared desire for all to have a better quality of life.

"Once any leadership position is accepted, this fundamental question emerges and presents itself to the new leader: How can our organization be better? *Unforgettable leaders solve problems and prevent problems. They make the area entrusted to them better.*"

Katy stated, "The job of a superintendent is to solve problems, and in doing so this will make the school district better."

Dr. Martin exclaimed, "That's it! And that is exactly what King Solomon did, Katy. He solved problems and improved the quality of life for those entrusted to his care."

Dr. Martin was in his ninth year of service to his school district. He worked well with the board of education, the community respected him, and his employees trusted him. Katy thought about the holistic responsibility of the superintendency and wrote in her journal:

The job of a superintendent is to make the school district better by solving its problems.

Dr. Martin continued, "In the book *The Road Less Traveled*, M. Scott Peck said, 'Life is difficult.' Peck explains that once people realize that life is difficult, then it is no longer difficult, because individuals understand and accept this truth, and come to expect that life presents a series of problems to solve. Each day, we can observe our leaders, whether at the local, state, or national level, as they discuss problems and seek solutions.

"Furthermore, the new superintendent will labor to answer this profound question: *What can the superintendent do to make the school district better and the community a better place to live?* A stellar school district makes economic development easier for those who work to create jobs.

"The superintendent leads the effort to improve student achievement by solving problems one at a time. Some are small problems that are quickly solved, while others are more complex and take longer to resolve. Unsolved problems will ultimately make their way to the superintendent's office! As President Harry Truman said, 'The buck stops here.' Now, this is what makes the superintendent position even more challenging day in and day out:

"The successful superintendent must solve problems in such a way as to make people feel good about the resolution of such problems. In other words, unforgettable superintendents solve problems and people embrace the pre-scribed plan of action. When this happens, it is because the leader solved the problem with wisdom."

Katy added this key thought to the notes in her journal:

Key Thought: The successful, unforgettable superintendent solves problems in such a way that people feel good about the resolution of such problems.

Dr. Martin continued, "The board of education wants problems solved with the least amount of controversy possible. They don't want multiple complaints registered to them through emails, texts, and phone calls. They want positive solutions. How does the leader find a positive solution? It is no easy assignment!

"As a high school principal, you know how to work with our central office staff, community leaders, parents, faculty, other school staff, and students on a daily basis in order to solve problems related to safety, academics, attendance, student discipline, athletics/extracurricular activities, special education, transportation, federal programs, the school breakfast and lunch program, the campus/facility, and personnel issues.

"As superintendent, a larger vision is required—a vision for the school district that will have a ripple effect throughout the city. The superintendent provides sound, carefully thought out recommendations to the board of education to move forward with corrective actions regarding students and personnel.

"Board members often provide a list of issues (problems to solve) to the new superintendent. Wise superintendents carefully listen and take copious notes during those initial planning meetings, and again when meeting individually with board members to get to know them and listen to their unique perspectives and concerns.

"There is a tremendous amount of responsibility in this key leadership role. Each decision the superintendent makes might possibly change or influence a number of lives. And the possibility that these decisions could result in potential litigation makes the thought process more important.

"It will be critical for the new superintendent to make wise decisions if he or she hopes to experience a long tenure in the superintendent's office—longer than the average two to three years in most school districts." Dr. Martin explained that he wanted to equip himself with the knowledge needed to be successful, and that is why he started focusing on the need for wisdom in his key leadership role.

After twenty-eight minutes, Dr. Martin said, "Our time is almost over today." His son's ball game would begin soon. Dr. Martin planned to attend the annual conference of the American Association of School Administrators (AASA) the next week, so he suggested meeting again in two weeks at Katy's school. The superintendent wanted to visit classrooms in the afternoon and meet afterward. Katy confirmed the suggested meeting time and place by nodding her head in agreement and saying, "Yes, this sounds good."

Dr. Martin continued, "Good. Now let's talk about your next assignment. Your assignment is two-fold. First, continue reading Proverbs and reflecting on its content and how it applies to your leadership role. Second, read about Solomon—the wise king who solved problems—in preparation for the next meeting."

Katy nodded in agreement and said, "Yes, and thank you, Dr. Martin."

MEETING AT THE HIGH SCHOOL

Dr. Martin enjoyed visiting classrooms at Independence High School two weeks later. When he walked through the halls and classrooms, everyone knew who he was. He was part of the team, not a stranger to the school. Even though he was a busy leader, he found time to make himself accessible through school visits, extracurricular activities, emails, and newsletters to employees. He spoke to the entire student body at least twice a year. He either gave an inspirational talk about character, citizenship, or scholarship, or he shared important information with students and staff about news in the school district.

It felt natural to have Dr. Martin in Katy's school, as he was an integral part of the Independence High School team. She was happy to meet with her mentor again, and felt relaxed when they completed their classroom visits and sat down at the conference table in her office to talk.

Dr. Martin began the conversation with a review—as all master teachers do. He said, "Do you remember the seven qualities of wise leaders we talked about during our last meeting?"

Katy said, "The first quality is vision, Dr. Martin. And another quality of wise leaders is that they seek counsel."

Dr. Martin said, "That's right. Wise leaders are visionary. They are seekers of knowledge, ethical, humble, and self-controlled. They seek counsel and strive to understand others."

Katy nodded in agreement and said, "It is beneficial to study Proverbs. Solomon's Proverbs make readers reflect on their decision-making process, and reflect more on the actions of self and others."

Dr. Martin smiled and said, "That is a true statement. Now let's talk about Solomon.

"The book of Proverbs is found in the Bible. The American Bible Society Survey of 2014 states that the Bible is America's number one favorite book. It is also the best-selling book of all time. In fact, this survey revealed that 88 percent of homes in America have a Bible. Leaders who want a double portion of wisdom as they seek the successful resolution of problems may wish to study Solomon's wise lessons.

"Proverbs is the book that holds 'the proverbs of Solomon, son of David, king of Israel: for attaining wisdom and discipline; for understanding and words of insight; for acquiring a disciplined and prudent life, doing what is right and just and fair' (Proverbs 1:1–3). Since the book of Proverbs has thirty-one chapters, the reader may wish to make it a practice to read one chapter a day in an effort to continually revisit the wisdom found within the chapters. Additionally, Solomon wrote the books of Ecclesiastes and Song of Solomon."

Katy knew that Proverbs was a book from the Bible, but had not read it in a long time. She said, "Dr. Martin, there aren't many people talking about the wisdom found in the Bible because some educators are afraid that it will get them into trouble talking about Scripture in a secular environment."

Dr. Martin said, "Katy, there is no law preventing the use of the Bible as a literary source."

Dr. Martin explained that educators are not allowed to proselytize in the public school setting, but all can learn and embrace practical truths from the Bible. He continued, "Even *Time* magazine acknowledged this fact in its April 2, 2007, publication. The cover of the magazine had a picture of the Bible with the caption: 'Why We Should Teach the Bible in Public School, but Very, Very Carefully.' This article explained that a well-educated person should be familiar with the writings within this treasured book."

Dr. Martin said, "So, who was Solomon, and how did his name become synonymous with wisdom?"

Katy replied, "Solomon was the son of Israel's King David. His greatest accomplishment was building the Holy Temple in Jerusalem. When he became king in approximately 967 BC, according to the Bible, God told him he would give Solomon anything he asked for, and Solomon asked for wisdom. He received the gift of wisdom and became the wisest man that ever lived."

Her mentor replied, "That's right, Katy. Look at the passage from the Bible in I Kings 3:5–13." He went to www.biblegateway.com to find this reading and began reading aloud. "It states":

> [5] At Gibeon the LORD appeared to Solomon during the night in a dream, and God said, "Ask for whatever you want me to give you."
> [6] Solomon answered, "You have shown great kindness to your servant, my father David, because he was faithful to you and righteous and upright in heart. You have continued this great kindness to him and have given him a son to sit on his throne this very day.
> [7] "Now, LORD my God, you have made your servant king in place of my father David. But I am only a little child and do not know how to carry out my duties.
> [8] Your servant is here among the people you have chosen, a great people, too numerous to count or number.
> [9] So give your servant a discerning heart to govern your people and to distinguish between right and wrong. For who is able to govern this great people of yours?"
> [10] The Lord was pleased that Solomon had asked for this.

¹¹ So God said to him, "Since you have asked for this and not for long life or wealth for yourself, nor have asked for the death of your enemies but for discernment in administering justice,

¹² I will do what you have asked. I will give you a wise and discerning heart, so that there will never have been anyone like you, nor will there ever be.

¹³ Moreover, I will give you what you have not asked for—both wealth and honor—so that in your lifetime you will have no equal among kings."

Dr. Martin continued, "Because Solomon was so wise, people would come from far away to seek his wisdom. The most famous story about Solomon's wisdom is about a child custody issue. In I Kings 3:16–28 the story is revealed. Do you mind reading this passage?" Dr. Martin refreshed the passage link on the website and quickly found the verses from I Kings 3. Katy began reading aloud:

¹⁶ Now two prostitutes came to the king and stood before him.

¹⁷ One of them said, "Pardon me, my lord. This woman and I live in the same house, and I had a baby while she was there with me.

¹⁸"The third day after my child was born, this woman also had a baby. We were alone; there was no one in the house but the two of us.

¹⁹ "During the night this woman's son died because she lay on him.

²⁰ "So she got up in the middle of the night and took my son from my side while I your servant was asleep. She put him by her breast and put her dead son by my breast.

²¹ "The next morning, I got up to nurse my son—and he was dead! But when I looked at him closely in the morning light, I saw that it wasn't the son I had borne."

²² The other woman said, "No! The living one is my son; the dead one is yours."

But the first one insisted, "No! The dead one is yours; the living one is mine." And so they argued before the king.

²³ The king said, "This one says, 'My son is alive and your son is dead,' while that one says, 'No! Your son is dead and mine is alive.'"

²⁴ Then the king said, "Bring me a sword." So they brought a sword for the king.

²⁵ He then gave an order: "Cut the living child in two and give half to one and half to the other."

²⁶ The woman whose son was alive was deeply moved out of love for her son and said to the king, "Please, my lord, give her the living baby! Don't kill him!" But the other said, "Neither I nor you shall have him. Cut him in two!"

²⁷ Then the king gave his ruling: "Give the living baby to the first woman. Do not kill him; she is his mother."

²⁸ When all Israel heard the verdict the king had given, they held the king in awe, because they saw that he had wisdom from God to administer justice.

Katy said, "Solomon brilliantly solved the problem in this well-known story. The two women came to the king to have him rule which one would legally claim the child. Solomon wisely told the women to split the baby in two pieces, since they both claimed the baby as their son. The biological mother screamed, 'No!' and this revealed to the king that she was indeed the mother because she would rather lose custody of the baby than have the baby killed by cutting it into two parts."

Dr. Martin said, "This is only one example of the wisdom displayed by Israel's King Solomon as he solved problems and rendered judgments. First century Jewish scholar Josephus said this about Solomon":

> The wisdom which God had bestowed upon Solomon was so great, that he exceeded the ancients, insomuch that he was no way inferior to the Egyptians, who are said to have been beyond all men in understanding. . . . He also excelled and distinguished himself in wisdom above those who were most eminent among the Hebrews at that time for shrewdness.

Katy said, "These stories reveal the wisdom Solomon possessed, Dr. Martin."

Dr. Martin's cell phone rang. As he listened to his caller, Katy wrote in her journal:

Solomon was a wise king. People came from far away to seek his wisdom.

Dr. Martin quickly completed his phone call and redirected his attention to his mentee. He told Katy to prepare for their next meeting, at which time they would examine the seven qualities of wise leaders, beginning with Quality #1: wise leaders are visionary. He said, "Dr. Carter, find a proverb or proverbs related to vision. Research Mr. Billy Coleman and discover what happened when he served as superintendent of a county school district. Be ready to discuss this superintendent's example of visionary leadership."

Katy looked forward to learning more about Billy Coleman and his story. She planned to search for proverbs related to vision and research Mr. Coleman later that night after supper.

Chapter One

Quality #1: Wise Leaders Are Visionary

Where there is no vision, the people perish. —Proverbs 29:18

After supper, Katy extracted a beautiful crystal glass from her china cabinet and filled it with crushed ice, water, and a slice of lemon. She laid a simple white linen napkin, edged with Nana Olive's ecru tatting, on her clean farm table to rest underneath the crystal glass so it could absorb any condensation. Then Katy retrieved her journal and quickly found the list of seven qualities of wise leaders listed on the fourth page.

An organized learner, she created a table of contents on the second page of her journal. Next, she numbered each page in the bottom right corner so she could easily reference her notes in the future. When she wanted to be able to find a particular page of notes, Katy simply titled the page and added the subject and page number to her Table of Contents.

Katy picked up her calligraphy pen, and in a beautiful black script she started a new section in her journal titled *Solomon.*

She listed these questions for reflection:

1. *Who was Solomon?*
2. *How did he become wise?*
3. *Where can his writings be found?*
4. *What is an example of his wise leadership and decision-making?*

Next, she created a new section in her journal:

Quality #1: Wise Leaders Are Visionary

Beneath the heading, she penned reflective questions to guide her in her quest for knowledge:

1. *What is visionary leadership?*

2. *Who is an example of a visionary leader? (Billy Coleman)*
3. *What did this person do to become a visionary leader?*
4. *How does this proverb relate to educational leadership standards?*

Then, she opened her laptop and began researching Mr. Billy Coleman with interest.

QUALITY #1: WISE LEADERS ARE VISIONARY

During Katy's next meeting with Dr. Martin he said, "Now, let's talk about the first quality of a wise leader: vision. Were you able to find any proverbs that related to vision, Katy?" Katy proudly replied, "Yes, in Proverbs 29:18, the King James Version states: *Where there is no vision, the people perish.*"

Dr. Martin replied, "Perfect, Katy. What did you learn about the visionary leader named Billy Coleman?"

Katy was eager to tell her mentor about Mr. Coleman, as she had thoroughly researched this leader. Katy looked at her notes and said, "Mr. Coleman, a retired high school principal, announced that he was running for election as superintendent of Cullman County Schools. He felt called to come out of retirement and help his beloved school system due to its dire financial situation. Long-time residents of the area, Billy and his wife, Shireen, are both educators. Mrs. Coleman is an elementary school educator and served as an elementary principal while Mr. Coleman served as a secondary teacher, coach, and high school principal."

Katy continued, "Mr. Coleman reached out to help his community for no reason other than to make it better. He didn't need a job. Listen to this letter to the editor about Mr. Coleman." Katy began reading the editorial:

> Billy Coleman, a true statesman, July 7, 2014
> King Solomon said, "Pride will ruin people, but those who are humble will be honored." He also said, "Where there is no vision, the people perish." Billy Coleman, the past elected superintendent of Cullman County Schools, is the living example of these wise statements of truth. A servant leader, Mr. Coleman blazed trails of improvement in the short time he served in this important leadership position.
> Recognizing the need for Cullman County Schools' financial stability, Billy extracted himself from the rank of retired principal, ran for the office of superintendent in 2010 on a platform of promised change, and delivered more than the citizens of Cullman expected. Once elected, he immediately charted the course for his vision, holding fifty-four town hall meetings about the need for a new half-cent sales tax dedicated to the children of Cullman County.
> Additionally, he talked about the need to change the county superintendent position from elected to appointed, and his desire to have the Section 16 lands committed to the oversight of Cullman County Schools. Mr. Coleman wisely

initiated a joint project, a shared Army–JROTC program, with Cullman City Schools to show unity in Cullman County. Together, the two districts promised to begin this program with revenue from the proposed half-cent sales tax.

In spite of the fact that 22 percent of this proposed tax would be promised to Cullman City Schools (based on student enrollment), he garnered undivided support for this new revenue source, securing its passage in the spring election of 2012. This new revenue, a welcomed relief from proration and Cullman County's depleted reserve fund, is already changing the landscape of education in his beloved school district.

Not one to rest on his laurels, Mr. Coleman continued his quest for Cullman County School District to control its Section 16 lands, gained legislative support and the support of Governor Bentley, and realized the unanimous passage of the legislature's act to allow the citizens of Cullman County to vote on this action in November of 2012—and it easily passed! Mr. Coleman also successfully persuaded his board of education and legislative delegation to change the position of superintendent from an elected to appointed position.

Mr. Coleman is courageous, patient, intelligent, and kind; he is a man of character. He is an excellent role model for young and old. He is more than a leader, more than a superintendent—Billy Coleman is a true statesman.

"That's the end of the editorial," Katy said.

Dr. Martin asked, "What did you learn about this leader after your review?"

Katy thought for a moment and said, "He is a visionary leader in that he saw that the school system could be better. Instead of grousing about the direction the school district was headed, which is what most people do, he left his comfortable retirement and got in the game! He had a plan, Dr. Martin, and he clearly communicated that plan to the community. The job of any leader is to solve problems to make their school system better. That's what Mr. Coleman did. He saw a problem—actually, several problems—and he created a plan to address the problems."

Dr. Martin said, "Nice job, Katy. You get an A+ on your assignment. You absolutely captured the essence of the job of any leader and Quality #1 of a wise leader—vision. Mr. Coleman sought the input of community leaders and citizens in order to make his vision a reality. He held fifty-four town meetings to discuss his plans and ideas and to seek input from the community. Mr. Coleman is a determined leader. Would you like to meet him?"

Katy enthusiastically replied, "Yes, it would be an honor to meet Mr. Billy Coleman." "Perhaps he can come for a visit," said Dr. Martin.

Dr. Martin asked, "Dr. Carter, are you a visionary leader? Do you have a plan for improvement? How will you seek input from stakeholders when you become a superintendent? How can you make your school district a better place for children to learn?"

Katy replied, "It is the goal of this superintendent candidate to be a visionary leader, but most days the immediate needs take priority. It seems there is always someone or some 'hot' issue demanding the principal's time and attention, like an angry parent waiting to see the principal, or a discipline or personnel issue to resolve."

Dr. Martin said, "All leaders can relate to your authentic answer, especially school leaders whose work with children can be more emotional as a result. It's difficult to be visionary."

Dr. Martin said, "The next quality to be discussed is knowledge. Wise leaders are seekers of knowledge. Wise leaders are aware of the political landscape. They avoid problems by addressing needs before they are asked to do so. Identify a seeker of knowledge and tell me about this leader when we meet again."

Katy said, "The information you are providing is enlightening, Dr. Martin. Thank you for providing this study of wise leadership. Would you like to meet at Independence High School after the homecoming pep rally in two weeks?"

Dr. Martin said, "That sounds like a plan. Homecoming promises to be an exciting week, as usual."

The next day, Katy found an email from Dr. Martin in her inbox. It read:

Dr. Carter,

It was a joy to visit Independence High School yesterday. It is evident that your professional, dedicated team is student centered. IHS master teachers display high expectations for their students. Thank you all for your continued pursuit of excellence in the classroom for our deserving students.

Sincerely,

Dr. Ron Martin

DR. CARTER AND DR. MARTIN
MEET WITH MR. COLEMAN

Independence High School, home of the Patriots, knew how to celebrate homecoming festivities. This year was extra special because it was the one-hundredth anniversary of the school. The student council had the original crest of the school captured in a lapel pin. Each student and employee received one of the commemorative pins, and there were an ample supply for members of the community, thanks to First National Bank covering the cost. Citizens and students were proudly displaying these celebratory pins on their shirts or lapels.

Independence High had a rich history of excellence, and businesses were easily convinced to support special events at the school. Even so, Dr. Carter was respectful of these business owners and careful not to take advantage of their generosity.

Numerous merchants allowed the school club members to paint their storefront windows with homecoming messages. The youthful, school-spirited painted windows provided a festive atmosphere in the small town of 14,000 inhabitants. Crimson and blue flooded the streets approaching the school campus, and inside the school the hallways were covered in homecoming memorabilia and event information.

Each club had a special bulletin board, and the student council hosted a bulletin board competition for creativity and school spirit. Community leaders judged the bulletin boards and five were selected as the best. Five businesses sponsored the cost of having the winning boards placed on billboards around town. Katy's favorite billboard was "Great Leaders Who Walked the Halls of IHS." She found this work to be inspiring to students because it showcased famous graduates and reminded students that they might become an astronaut or mayor or congressman one day.

Dr. Martin was the biggest supporter of IHS. He played football when he was in high school and college. He and his wife, Brenda, could be found at most games along with their son and daughter. Their daughter, Mary, looked so cute dressed as a junior cheerleader. She was the most enthusiastic supporter of the Patriots, even if she was only eight years old. Their oldest child, John, was ten years old. He played little league football through the city and recreation program. The entire family embraced school events and made them a part of family life. Their closets were filled with crimson and blue clothes.

Dr. Martin arrived at the pep rally wearing a smart-looking Patriot pullover sweater. Beneath it, a starched white shirt peeked out along with a crimson and blue plaid bowtie. An intelligent and kind leader, he took pride in his appearance, and, as such, the board of education and stakeholders were proud to have Dr. Martin represent the school district in any capacity. He dressed professionally and appropriately and was prepared to be on the evening news or speak at the local Rotary club at any given moment.

The superintendent stood beside the principal during the pep rally. The marching band was energetically belting out the latest halftime tunes, while the cheerleaders and majorettes happily provided dances perfectly in sync with the beat. The football players were now seated in the bleachers, looking stoic after their grand entrance initiated by Liberty the Lion, their mascot. Liberty came running into the gym wildly waving the American flag. The football players, walking in an authoritative, confident manner, were cool and composed. They looked strong and mean.

The students cheered wildly as the homecoming court was announced during the exuberant pep rally. Excitement continued to mount after the conclusion of the alma mater as visiting parents and students whispered about who they predicted would be crowned homecoming queen at the football game later that night. While the members of the Key Club helped the custodians collect streamers and debris from the rousing pep rally, Dr. Carter escorted Dr. Martin to her office.

When they arrived, the junior class president, Mack Howard, was waiting there with two boxed mum corsages in his hands. He said, "Dr. Carter, Dr. Martin, on behalf of the junior class, this is a small token of appreciation to each of you. Dr. Martin, we thought Mrs. Martin would enjoy wearing this homecoming corsage at tonight's game. And we know that Dr. Carter would enjoy wearing one!" Both leaders smiled broadly and thanked this thoughtful student leader.

Cynthia, the school secretary, handed Dr. Martin and Dr. Carter bottles of cold water, knowing they must be thirsty after the pep rally. In unison they both replied, "Thank you, Mrs. Perkins." Cynthia told Katy there was a gentleman waiting to see her. Katy was deeply disappointed, but didn't show it, because she had been looking forward to talking to her mentor at this time.

However, her disappointment quickly disappeared when she discovered the identity of her guest. The gentleman stood up and walked toward them, smiled at the principal, and said, "You must be Dr. Carter."

Katy replied, "Yes, that's right."

The gentleman said, "My name is Billy Coleman."

Katy exclaimed, "What an honor it is for me to meet you, sir! Please come in. What a wonderful surprise, Dr. Martin! Would you like a bottled water?"

Mr. Coleman said, "Thank you, that would be nice."

Dr. Martin shook hands with Mr. Coleman and said, "Thank you for joining us today. It's good to see you, and it is an honor to have you here. How is Shireen?"

As Katy directed them to her office, Mr. Coleman said, "Thank you, but the pleasure is all mine. Shireen and the boys are fine. They are grown up with families of their own now. Is everyone well at your home?"

Dr. Martin said, "Yes, thank you."

After Mr. Coleman encouraged Dr. Carter in her aspiration to become a superintendent, Dr. Martin quickly gave an overview of their study of Proverbs and leadership, according to Solomon. Katy said, "Wise leaders share seven qualities: They are visionary. They are seekers of knowledge, and they are ethical. They are humble and self-controlled. They seek advice. They understand others."

Dr. Martin pronounced, "Well stated, Dr. Carter. Solomon said, 'Where there is no vision, the people perish.' Dr. Carter researched your legacy as a visionary superintendent."

Mr. Coleman looked down and humbly said, "The outcomes were a result of a team effort. Billy Coleman doesn't deserve all the credit."

Katy interjected, "The outcomes are impressive, Mr. Coleman. You stated your vision and worked diligently to bring each part of your vision to life."

Mr. Coleman ran for election with a three-part plan to rescue the district from its financial plight and improve its condition. He recommended a tax increase, taking control of Section 16 lands that lay within the district's county lines, and he recommended that the superintendent position be changed from an elected position to an appointed one. He clearly articulated a vision for making his school district better.

Mr. Coleman said, "Solomon is right. Vision is vital. It is essential—not just to a school system, but to a nation, and, maybe just as much, to an individual." He was passionate when Katy emphasized that leaders must see clearly where they are going, but just as importantly, they must see who they are. "If they forget who they are, what they believe in and what they stand for, then direction has no meaning. To go anywhere, there must be a clearly defined starting point. That is where the vision begins."

Mr. Coleman continued, "In today's world, people are desperately searching for leadership—leadership that doesn't compromise integrity and honesty, no matter what the cost." Mr. Coleman told Katy and Dr. Martin about the student leadership initiative in their school district. The students looked at current leaders, and leaders from past generations, and discussed the positive differences they made, hopefully realizing the sacrifices of past generations that enabled the students to enjoy the rights and privileges of the present.

Mr. Coleman said, "As students take a close look at the founding fathers of the United States of America, they are reminded of the beliefs and values this great nation was founded on and how those values must not be compromised and certainly not forgotten. Past leaders paid for America's freedom with a very dear price. Perhaps this sentiment is captured with the saying, 'All gave some; some gave all.'"

Mr. Coleman explained that their students were challenged to search out those beliefs and values upon which they could build their lives. Realizing that these values might be challenged and questioned, students discussed how to be strong enough to never compromise their beliefs. Mr. Coleman said, "That is the beginning of leadership and the starting point for the visionary journey. Likewise, stakeholders need to know what the school system believes in, and just as important, to know those values and beliefs will not be compromised. That is where a *vision* for the school system begins."

Katy asked, "Why did you want to leave retirement to get involved when the financial situation was so bleak for your school district?"

Mr. Coleman explained that he came out of retirement because he wanted to do his part to help their school district. Their district had a unity that revolved around a very sacred core of values, and one of those values was a commitment to young people. Cullman County had been recently chosen as the number one place in the state to raise children, and he felt that recognition was a testimony to the emphasis placed on guiding young people down a path that led to success.

When he became superintendent he was told more than once it was the worst possible time to be superintendent. This was not because their district was going through unique problems, but because the economy was at one of the lowest points in American history. Times were tough, and for school systems whose funds were based to a large degree on sales tax, they were especially bad.

When Mr. Coleman began as superintendent, their school system had only a five-day fund balance. State law required that school systems have a thirty-day or one-month fund balance. The state required systems with less than a one-month fund balance to create a plan for improvement, and when he attended the first meeting to develop a plan—only weeks into his first year as superintendent—the room was full. During that first year the district's fund balance went from five days to twenty-four days. Today they have a forty-five-day fund balance, thanks to a lot of people making a lot of sacrifices.

SHORT-TERM GOAL: TAX INCREASE

As the district faced economic challenges, Mr. Coleman said they needed a short-term and a long-term plan to bring about stability. The short-term plan was proposing a half-cent sales tax increase, to be voted on by the people. This proposal was voted down a few years before, so it would obviously be an uphill battle. Of course, the easiest solution would have been to persuade the county commission to impose the tax, but Mr. Coleman believed it was important to win the support of the people.

The vote was set for the spring. During the six months preceding the vote, Billy Coleman held fifty-four public meetings to share the school district's vision for how those funds would be spent. He and his team presented facts that showed local funding for school systems in the state, and where their school district ranked in the state as well as in comparison to surrounding systems. He showed where the needs were and how a half-cent sales tax increase would help meet those needs. He pointed out that the city system would receive their small portion of the new tax revenue based on student enrollment, and that the two systems would partner on starting a new ROTC program with part of the additional funds.

The vote passed in the spring of 2012, and it was the first time in history that the people in Cullman County voted for any kind of tax increase. Since the passing of the tax, the funds generated have been used exactly as promised. Mr. Coleman told Katy he was thankful to the people for that vote of support for their young people.

LONG-TERM GOAL:
CONTROL OF SECTION 16 LANDS

With the passing of the half-cent sales tax, Mr. Coleman and his team turned their attention to their long-term financial challenge. For several years, the school district had not been able to address capital projects due to lack of funds. Like all school systems, there were facility needs that became urgent when the student population increased and when old buildings needed to be replaced. This plan was way out there—definitely "outside the box." It had never been tried before, but that is what makes for an exciting story.

In the Land Ordinance of 1785, before Alabama became a state, the federal government designated one section out of every township to be set aside for public schools. Even today Section 16 land exists. For the most part, Section 16 land was used for timber cutting and leased to hunting clubs. Much of Section 16 land has disappeared, sometimes being actually used for schools and sometimes not. In the beginning, Cullman County had twenty Section 16 lands; today there are only three left.

In the Alabama Constitution of 1901, Mobile County School System was allowed to manage their Section 16 property. Other than that one school system, no other system had ever had ownership rights over Section 16 property!

The state of Alabama appointed the Conservation Department to oversee and manage the use of Section 16 property for a 10 percent management fee. Revenue that was produced was placed into a trust in Montgomery, and school systems in the state received yearly funds from the interest earned in the trust. A lawsuit several years ago made it mandatory for school systems to receive all funds derived from Section 16 properties in their school districts. Those funds could no longer be divided with schools in other counties.

Mr. Coleman said, "Cullman County has three Section 16 properties. Two of those are traditional pieces in that they are probably best used for timber and hunting leases. But one of those pieces is the full 640 acres that happens to be on Smith Lake, a man-made lake. There was no Smith Lake when the Land Ordinance of 1785 was established, so some of the acreage is under water, but 435 acres is absolutely above water."

"It contains over 26,000 feet of shoreline and is some of the most beautiful property on the lake. Now this property's value certainly goes beyond that of hunting clubs and timberland, and it became the goal to secure Section 16 property right in Cullman County for Cullman County Schools."

Katy asked, "How did you go through all the red tape to secure this land, Mr. Coleman?"

Mr. Coleman explained that they held a meeting with representatives from the Conservation Department and the State Department of Education,

1

who reminded them that no school system had ever gained ownership rights to Section 16 land and that nobody ever would.

Mr. Coleman and his team argued that these lands were given to public schools and the local school system should manage the property. At that time the economy was tough, and this property, if it were managed properly, could be a long-term answer to funding desperately needed capital projects in their system. Many systems had tried to secure this property and were told the same thing. But Mr. Coleman was not quitting. He decided to try to meet with the governor.

Mr. Coleman was thankful that the governor took time out of his busy schedule to listen to a small group of "outside the box" thinkers from a rural school district. The team came to the meeting prepared with maps, charts, and a plan—a vision—and explained that if they were allowed to manage this property, they would put only 10 percent of any proceeds from Section 16 property into the general fund. The rest would be placed in a trust in Cullman County and each year the school district would use only the interest generated by the trust, thereby making the funding source last forever.

The governor liked the idea and commended the team for their creative problem-solving proposal: finding an existing resource and developing it for a long-term solution. Standing on the front steps of the capitol building, Mr. Coleman told his team that if this plan became a reality he would dance at a board meeting.

Katy was sitting on the edge of her seat, listening intently. She asked, "What happened next, Mr. Coleman?"

Mr. Coleman visited the city school board and explained to them the plan and that they would receive 17 percent of the interest of the trust based on the students that lived in their district. The county would receive 83 percent. They were not aware of the Section 16 story, but they were supportive of the plan.

Then they shared the plan with their legislative delegation. They were a key component to helping the school district. They would propose legislation calling for a vote to allow the school district to have ownership rights over Section 16 properties in Cullman County. Now here was the kicker. If one state legislator—one—voted against this proposed local piece of legislation, it would require a statewide vote. If the vote were unanimous, then another vote would take place in Cullman County.

Mr. Coleman was confident the people of Cullman County would vote for the proposal, but getting the whole state to support it created a whole different dynamic. At 11:50 p.m., literally ten minutes before the legislative session ended, he got the call from Senator Paul Bussman.

The bill had passed unanimously and the vote would be held in Cullman County! The next step was educating the people on Section 16 land and how allowing the school system to manage it was a good thing. Like the sales tax initiative, more than fifty meetings were held.

Obviously, this was a much easier sell than the sales tax vote. This was land set aside for schools and would be of no cost to anyone. Pictures of the property were displayed, and it was easy to see the potential this wonderful property possessed. The team did not, however, take anything for granted. Donated funds provided ads and yard signs. No school funds were used in any of their efforts to get the word out. The vote passed easily and Cullman County became the first school system in Alabama to seek and secure management rights for Section 16 property, joining only Mobile County Schools, who received their rights in the constitution of 1901.

Mr. Coleman said his dance would probably never be considered a great dance, but it met the standards of a "happy dance" when he was reminded of his promise to dance at a board meeting if his plan became a reality. He said he would treasure the sound of laughter and celebration in the room during that special board meeting.

Dr. Martin laughed and said, "Outstanding job, Mr. Coleman!"

Mr. Coleman replied, "Thank you, Ronnie. It was a team effort that required the hard work of many wonderful people who believed in this dream, and the support of the fine people of Cullman County who voted for it."

Katy was immersed in his story and wanted to hear more, but as she looked at her watch she realized she would soon need to get ready for the football game. She said, "Mr. Coleman, please tell me about how you led the effort to change the superintendent position from an elected to an appointed position."

Mr. Coleman told Katy that at his first board meeting after being elected as superintendent, he told the board that if they ever thought about the possibilities of having an appointed superintendent instead of an elected one, now might be a good time. He believed the appointing of a superintendent was a better process than electing a superintendent, and he would lead the effort to change the process if they desired.

Mr. Coleman conveyed that superintendents are not politicians; they are educators. They do not have the time or money to run for re-election, and they don't want to risk compromising the job they do. Therefore, they should not have to make decisions based on how people vote. For example, in some cases, a sitting elected superintendent is defeated in an election and that presents an extremely awkward transition process. There were only three states with elected superintendents. His state had less than a third of the superintendents elected.

As it turned out, the board was interested in the process, so they worked together to change the position. The first step was to allow the people of Cullman County to vote on whether the position would be elected or appointed. He asked one of their legislators to propose that referendum, but as it turns out, he requested a statewide vote and, of course, that did not even get out of committee.

Their state has some very large school systems with elected superintendents and perhaps that is why that effort was doomed from its inception. The only other alternative was for the board to ask their legislative delegation to pass a law making the position appointed, which they did. This did not happen without much discussion.

Obviously, some wanted the superintendent position to remain elected, but there was strong support for an appointed superintendent. In the last three years, as people had become more familiar with the process and had their questions answered, many came to appreciate the integrity of the process of finding a qualified, appointed superintendent.

So the position was changed, as a result of their legislative delegation's leadership. Today Mr. Coleman's school system has an appointed superintendent.

Katy said, "Do you mind sharing why you didn't apply for the position? You obviously had a tremendous amount of influence and support."

Billy explained that he was asked to apply on more than one occasion. He did not apply for the job because he ran for election on a platform that included changing the position, and he did not want people to think he supported it so he could get it.

Mr. Coleman said, "Today the perception is strong that those in leadership positions always have an ulterior motive, always working behind the scenes for things that center on their own self-interest. There is a lack of trust for decision-makers for those very reasons. There seems to always be a hidden agenda. True leadership revolves around being a servant and doing what is best for others."

Dr. Martin said, "This is a belief Mr. Coleman models in his daily walk. He is an authentic servant leader."

Mr. Coleman said, "The appointed superintendent opportunity was best for the system. It was not then nor should it ever be about Billy Coleman. It was a blessing to not have plans to apply."

Mr. Coleman shared that when they started the process, they found out the best time to hire an appointed superintendent was in the summer. So, he decided to retire six months early to accommodate that timetable. He enjoyed helping the new superintendent transition into this key leadership position.

Dr. Martin said, "Mr. Coleman, thank you for taking time to come and share your story today. Is there anything else you want to share about vision with Dr. Carter?"

Mr. Coleman said, "It has been a pleasure to be with you both. Every effort certainly starts with a vision, but there must be a commitment to pursue that vision. The world is full of dreamers, but many are dreamers dedicated to making those dreams come true. That is where the separation lies. *The three dreams discussed today happened not because an individual dreamed them but because a group of people believed in the dream and worked hard to make it happen. Communicating the dream so others can take ownership is one of the secrets to making dreams come true."*

Dr. Martin said, "Now that is a profound statement of truth."

As they concluded the meeting Dr. Martin asked Mr. Coleman if he and his wife, Shireen, would be able to attend the football game.

Billy said, "Yes, there is nothing more enjoyable than football on a Friday night. Shireen went shopping while we met. We will meet you at the game."

Dr. Carter said, "Please come up to the press box for a snack, especially during halftime to watch the Patriot marching band perform. Did you know the band earned superior ratings at the state competition last month?"

Mr. Coleman said, "That is fantastic!"

Before Mr. Coleman left he shared his favorite proverb (from Proverbs 15:22) with the two leaders: "Plans fail for lack of counsel, but with many advisors they succeed."

Dr. Martin claimed this as one of his favorite proverbs, also. Mr. Coleman said good-bye and left the office to go meet his wife.

Dr. Martin turned to Katy and asked, "Would you like to talk about Quality #2 next Wednesday following the principals' meeting?"

Katy said that worked with her schedule and added that it was a wonderful surprise to actually meet Billy Coleman face-to-face. She thanked her mentor for inviting Mr. Coleman to come visit. She knew she would never forget his amazing, inspiring story of visionary leadership.

Her mentor replied, "Now it is your turn to find a living example of wise leadership. Come prepared to tell me about a leader who seeks knowledge, and look for proverbs related to this second quality."

Katy said, "Yes, sir."

Before Katy left her office she sent Mr. Coleman an email and copied Dr. Martin on it. It read:

Mr. Coleman,

Thank you for taking time to come to Independence High School today to share valuable lessons about wise leadership. You are a visionary leader who has made an indelible impression on this school leader's professional life. It was an honor to meet you and have you visit Independence High School.

With gratitude,

Katy Carter

Katy then sent another email to Dr. Martin:

Dr. Martin,

Thank you for bringing Mr. Coleman to Independence High School today. This was an excellent opportunity to learn about visionary leadership through his living example. Thank you for mentoring this aspiring superin-tendent.

With respect, appreciation, and admiration,
Katy

Chapter Two

Quality #2: Wise Leaders Are Seekers of Knowledge

Pay attention and listen to the sayings of the wise. —Proverbs 22:17

On Saturday, during Katy's early morning quiet time, she thought about her meeting with Mr. Coleman and Dr. Martin the day before. She considered the time they shared to be a treasured gift fondly remembered. She reflected upon the homecoming football game and all of its festivities. Even though this high school principal was pleased with the outcome of this widely celebrated event, she asked herself, "What was the highlight of homecoming week? What aspects of the event could be improved?"

Upon further consideration of the week's activities, Dr. Carter mentally answered each question. The pep rally could have been longer. They ran out of time when they recognized the homecoming court. However, everyone respectfully stayed in place even when the bell rang. She was proud of her students as they waited to be dismissed properly by the student council president, who served as the emcee of the event.

The high school widely distributed 4,000 of the one-hundredth anniversary commemorative pins to stakeholders, students, and staff. The beautiful pin would be a pleasant reminder of the celebration each time it was worn. It definitely served as a highlight of homecoming, along with the fun memories that were made at the pep rally, parade, bonfire, football game, and dance.

With a hot cup of coffee in her hands, Katy walked to her bedroom and looked at the classic pin displayed on her dresser. She proudly admired the crest as unexpected tears quietly spilled down her cheeks, revealing her gratitude for the honor of serving as Independence High School's principal. She was thankful for her education and the opportunities it afforded, and welcomed the cloak of responsibility presented to her.

Katy wiped her warm, salty tears away with a white linen handkerchief that was tucked in the right pocket of her chenille robe. This was only one of the numerous handmade gifts Katy received from Nana Olive, who loved to smock, tat, and crochet. The tiny, delicate pink crocheted loops surrounding the handkerchief served as a reminder to Katy of the precious details of her life. Katy returned to the kitchen and opened the refrigerator door to glance at her homecoming mum corsage. It was sweet of the class officers to provide a mum corsage for her to wear. Katy loved her students with all her heart.

Katy saw the microwave's digital clock, and it reminded her that it was time for her morning ritual of reading a chapter in Proverbs. As she read at the kitchen table, she made notes in her journal about the chapter, and then started thinking about the second quality of wise leaders. Dr. Martin said that wise leaders were seekers of knowledge. On the next page of her journal, she created a new section in black calligraphy:

Quality #2: Wise Leaders Are Seekers of Knowledge
Beneath it she wrote the following goals she established for herself:

1. *To be a seeker of knowledge (lifelong learner) throughout life,*
2. *To have an open mind,*
3. *To read widely, and*
4. *To seek new ideas by observing successful practices and listening to others in professional learning lectures or conversations.*

Katy often used the phrase "seeker of knowledge" to describe herself. She loved learning new ideas and better ways to improve her life and the lives of those entrusted to her care. Katy searched and found two proverbs related to seeking knowledge and carefully captured these verses in her journal:

1. *I, wisdom, dwell together with prudence; I possess knowledge and discretion.* —Proverbs 8:12
2. *Pay attention and listen to the sayings of the wise.* —Proverbs 22:17

Katy knew several colleagues who were also seekers of knowledge. Aren't all educators seekers of knowledge? She effortlessly produced the names of three respected colleagues who were lifelong learners. She often shared conversations with them about the latest book in the education arena or an innovative idea gleaned from a professional journal or conference.

But one leader rose above the others. Dr. Barry Carroll was not only a seeker himself; he took others with him on his journey to learn. Dr. Carroll created opportunities for those he supervised to learn from books, knowledgeable speakers, and each other. Katy remembered the professional learning communities he created as an administrator in her school district, and she knew about the learning opportunities he created in his current role as super-intendent.

When Katy completed her research, she emailed Dr. Carroll to schedule a time to talk to him. Then she dressed in her Saturday attire: jeans, a favorite Independence High School sweatshirt over a white turtleneck, and gray boots. After putting beef stew in her crockpot, Katy prepared to go for a twenty-minute walk. She texted her neighbor and invited Tessa, a beautiful golden retriever, to go with her on her walk.

Katy embraced the sunshine, and took a deep breath of the fresh air as she stepped outside. She briskly walked along the neighborhood sidewalks with Tessa at her side. Katy stopped to pick up a piece of trash and place it in a rolled up grocery bag she brought with her. She used the pause as an opportunity to pet this sweet therapy dog. Tessa loved the attention and morning walk.

When Katy returned, she was refreshed from the sunshine, exercise, and time with Tessa. She created a list for the grocery store, prepared a thermos of ice water, and left for a day of errands and a fun lunch with her childhood friend, Gena. Katy looked forward to the weekends. She enjoyed them tremendously because she worked hard during the week. She eagerly sought time for rest and play on the weekend. The weekends were a time for restoration for Katy.

On Monday, Katy successfully connected with Dr. Carroll via telephone. It was an enlightening conversation, one that she looked forward to sharing with Dr. Martin. When Katy met with her mentor, she found the lessons to be thought provoking and uplifting, and they helped to confirm her decision to seek the superintendency in order to affect the lives of students in a positive manner. The position felt like a natural next step for Katy even though she was quite happy serving as a high school principal.

After the principals' meeting on Wednesday, Katy went to Dr. Martin's office for her scheduled appointment with her mentor. Beth Robertson, Dr. Martin's executive secretary, looked up when she entered the office suite and smiled. "Dr. Martin will be with you shortly, Dr. Carter," Beth stated. She asked, "Would you like a cup of coffee?"

Katy replied, "Thank you. That would be nice." After she received a cup of hot coffee in a black mug with the school system's logo on the front, the superintendent opened his door and invited her in to start their meeting.

As they walked to the conference table Katy said, "Dr. Martin, thank you again for arranging the meeting with Mr. Coleman, a visionary leader."

Dr. Martin said, "He certainly is an inspiring individual. It was a wonderful meeting and time of fellowship at the football game. And the Patriots won the homecoming football game!"

Dr. Martin commended Katy for the nice email she sent Mr. Coleman. He told her that she had the gift of noticing the efforts of other people and displaying gratitude, and that is a rare gift. Katy smiled and said, "Thank you, Dr. Martin."

As they sat down, Ronnie handed Katy an envelope and said, "Please take this letter commending the Independence High School student council, faculty, and staff for a stellar one-hundredth anniversary homecoming."

Dr. Martin added, "The commemorative pins with the school crest and the creative window paintings in the community were exceptional. Bravo, Dr. Carter!"

Katy was touched by his acknowledgment of their hard work. She reached for the letter with tears in her eyes. "Thank you, Dr. Martin. Your thoughtful letter will be appreciated."

Dr. Martin paused and then said, "Now, let's review. We talked about the job description for a leader, and we talked about Solomon and his proverbs. We discussed "Quality #1: Wise Leaders are Visionary." And today we will talk about "Quality #2: Wise Leaders are Seekers of Knowledge." Do you remember the other five qualities of wise leaders?"

Katy replied, "Yes. Wise leaders are ethical, humble, and self-controlled. Wise leaders seek counsel and they seek to understand others."

"That's correct. Good job, Katy. Wise leaders are seekers of knowledge who stay one step ahead because they are lifelong learners. They learn through education and reflection on experiences. Because these wise leaders are knowledgeable about the latest research and laws, they stay ahead. Wise leaders seek continual improvement through learning. They use learning to help them in their quest to prevent and solve problems day in and day out. They often ask themselves, 'How can this area be improved or more effective?'"

Then Dr. Martin asked, "Did you find proverbs related to knowledge?"

Katy replied, "Yes. Initially, in Proverbs 8:12, Solomon says, 'I, wisdom, dwell together with prudence; I possess knowledge and discretion.' And in Proverbs 22:17 Solomon writes, 'Pay attention to the sayings of the wise.'"

Dr. Martin interjected, "To be prudent means to be careful in action or in providing for the future. Wise leaders are watchful; they carefully guard what is entrusted to their care. They obtain knowledge through research, books, experiences, and through talking to others in similar circumstances. And, yes, they do pay attention to what wise people share with them."

Dr. Martin continued, "Seekers of knowledge are planners. Rather than solve a major problem after it occurs, they look for proactive ways to operate so that the problem is avoided. They solve problems in advance by simply avoiding them. For example, wise principals create supervision schedules in order to avoid problems in assemblies and class changes. They invest time in *preventing* an altercation rather than *resolving* an issue afterwards. Because seekers of knowledge are prudent, they are good at solving problems before they arise."

Katy replied, "That is true." After talking to the leader who exemplifies Quality #2, the following proverbs were added:

3. *The prudent see danger and take refuge.* —Proverbs 27:12
4. *A man who remains stiff-necked after many rebukes will suddenly be destroyed—without remedy.* —Proverbs 29:1."

Katy continued, "In the National Education Association's "Code of Ethics," it states: *The educator, believing in the worth and dignity of each human being, recognizes the supreme importance of the pursuit of truth, devotion to excellence, and the nurture of the democratic principles.* These proverbs speak truth."

Dr. Martin said, "When truth is recognized, it can be seen in different arenas. Who did you identify as a seeker of knowledge?"

Katy said, "His name is Dr. Barry Carroll."

Dr. Martin said, "Yes, he is a fine fellow; he formerly served as a principal and director in our school district before becoming a superintendent. Dr. Carroll is indeed a seeker of knowledge. He is a lifelong learner who creates new programs and looks for innovative methods to conduct business. Tell me more about Dr. Carroll."

THE CASE OF DR. BARRY CARROLL

Katy said, "In searching for the name of a leader who exemplified lifelong learning, several names emerged, but Barry Carroll's name rose to the top of the list because Dr. Carroll not only continues to learn himself, *he takes others with him on his journey to seek knowledge.* Dr. Barry Carroll created the Aspiring Administrator Academy and the Aspiring Superintendents Academy several years ago when he was employed by Washington County. Dr. Carroll was a seeker of knowledge then and now."

Katy told her mentor about her phone conference with Dr. Carroll. He graciously agreed to discuss these professional learning initiatives. Katy asked him for permission to record their conversation and he agreed. She asked Dr. Martin, "Would you like to hear our brief phone conversation?"

Katy's mentor nodded his head in agreement and said, "Yes."

Katy extracted her small recorder and pressed play as she placed it on the table. Dr. Carroll's gentle voice began talking:

Interviewing for administrative positions can be an interesting, exciting, and exhausting process. During the interview for the position of superintendent, several questions were asked during the interview that caused me to think, "Why are they asking that question?" The most interesting question posed during the board interview was, "If selected as superintendent, how will you increase the pool of applicants for administrative positions in the district?"

Dr. Carroll told the board members that he would increase the pool of applicants in two ways. First, he planned to develop a program designed to identify prospective leaders within the school district. He planned to train participants and to encourage them to become certified in administration. Second, he recommended recruiting seasoned administrators with varied backgrounds and experience outside of the school district in order to diversify the administrative team. Dr. Carroll believed his answer to that question was a major factor in being selected to serve.

The first week after Dr. Carroll became superintendent, he learned that there was a vacant principal position. He learned that the position was posted and advertised. He anticipated the search would yield twenty-five to thirty applicants. To his surprise and disappointment, when he asked for the applicant file, he found only two applications in it. It was at that moment that he knew he had to create the program he described in his interview. They had to develop potential leaders within the district because the number of leaders was diminishing, if not perishing.

Katy's voice was heard on the recording asking, "How did you create the program, Dr. Carroll?"

In a sincere voice he described the quality professional development program he called the "Aspiring Administrator Academy." The idea was promoted within their district, and an inspired class of participants were selected and trained in critical areas of administration.

Through much planning and assistance from a number of quality educators, the vision came to fruition during the ten years of Dr. Carroll's service as superintendent. Dr. Carroll said, "The Board later realized the school district had many potential leaders within the district. It simply took encouragement and a structured program for them to step forward and blossom into confident administrative leaders who could lead the district into the future."

Katy asked, "How many educators participated in the program?"

Dr. Carroll answered, "In the first year of the Aspiring Administrator Academy (AAA), the program began with an overwhelming response from forty potential leaders who applied. After an intense vetting process, twenty-five applicants were selected who best fit the program and set a high standard for selecting administrators in the district. This cohort group would become the foundation for administrative leadership in the district."

Dr. Carroll explained that he made the Aspiring Administrator Academy one of his top priorities. He became deeply involved in the selection of topics, presenters, and activities for the program. At the first Aspiring Administrator Academy meeting, he communicated the vision for the program and for the district. The twenty-five class members responded with an overwhelming commitment to the program, a desire to learn, and a shared vision to resolve the issue of too few leaders in the district.

The Aspiring Administrator Academy was designed to be a one-year program that included approximately ten daylong meetings. Topics included the following:

- Finance and Budgeting
- School Law
- Instructional Leadership
- Safety and Security
- Human Resources
- Student Services
- Politics in Education
- Decision-Making
- High School Athletics
- Federal Programs
- Media Relations
- Technology in the Classroom
- Team Building
- Interview Skills
- Other topics related to current issues and trends

Dr. Carroll said, "The program was intense, but fun. By the end of the first year, the twenty-five class members bonded and became a support group who would evangelize the district's vision and mission. Since the participants were from different schools, they shared the common messages with their colleagues and, hopefully, inspired some of them to participate in future Academy cohorts."

Dr. Carroll said, "At the end of each year, participants determined if administration and instructional leadership was the right career path for them. Some participants went back to graduate school to earn a degree or certification in administration. Those who were already certified were encouraged to apply for positions within the district. A few participants decided that administration and instructional leadership might not be a career path for them, but each expressed the benefits that would help them become a stronger leader in the positions they currently held."

"How was the program evaluated?" Katy inquired.

Dr. Carroll replied, "The Academy was evaluated by participants and presenters. Based on the results of the evaluations, adjustments to the program were made for the following year. The program expanded to include more topics and activities, such as school visits with proven school leaders, a mentoring program, a ropes course for team building, and other topics of interest."

Katy asked, "Is there anything else you want to share about the Aspiring Administrator Academy?"

Dr. Carroll said, "Yes, the Aspiring Administrator Academy not only fulfilled the original vision, but served as a common bond for teachers and administrators throughout the district. In addition, the Aspiring Administrator Academy served as a platform to create ideas, test theories, and promote student, teacher, and administrator success. Participants became a family, which led to their district motto, '*We are a school system, not a system of schools.*'"

Dr. Carroll explained that the Aspiring Administrator Academy began with a vision for increasing leadership capacity to plug the hole of diminishing leaders within the school district, and the results were stunning. The AAA graduates continue to be selected for administrative and instructional leadership positions, both within the district and in other school districts. The program continues to have a dramatic impact on the lives of those who participated.

Katy said, "Congratulations on creating this successful program. You are to be commended for your leadership and efforts."

Dr. Carroll replied, "Thank you, Dr. Carter. It was a team effort. We were pleased that the evaluations of the program indicated our first AAA was a tremendous success. It was an honor to play a part in the development and professional growth of these future leaders. Research reveals that student achievement increases when district leaders and educators embrace professional learning." Dr. Carroll said that because of this, in his school district administrators and teachers sought continual learning. However, they were careful to learn in moderation, after observing districts that overloaded their team members with constant change.

Katy understood the importance of learning and changing in moderation. There are only 24 hours in a day, and 168 hours in a week. Teachers must incorporate learning into their daily schedules, but not be frustrated with never-ending initiatives based upon such learning. Katy's voice was heard in the recording saying, "Thank you for taking time to discuss the Aspiring Administrator Academy with me today, Dr. Carroll."

Katy turned the recorder off and laid a sheet of paper on the table. She said, "Would you like to hear the key points from Dr. Carroll's story?"

Dr. Martin replied, "Yes, what are your takeaways?"

Katy said, "After examining Dr. Carroll's work, I found that the three key points that are in concert with the proverbs are:

1. Dr. Carroll saw 'danger' ahead. That is, he saw, firsthand, the lack of applicants for administrative openings in his district. Therefore, he made a plan. He created a refuge for those who might be interested in administrative positions. It was safe to 'try it out.'
   The prudent see danger and take refuge. —Proverbs 27:12

2. Dr. Carroll's future administrators listened to and learned from successful presenters about administrative roles and responsibilities. These individuals possessed a degree of wisdom, or they would not have been selected by Dr. Carroll to speak to his future administrators. *Pay attention and listen to the sayings of the wise.* —Proverbs 22:17

3. Dr. Carroll was smart to not forget about the question his board member posed when he interviewed for the superintendent position. Had he ignored the question, it could have created a problem for him later. Board members wish to be heard when they define problems. Furthermore, they expect resolutions to problems. This relates to the proverb, *A man who remains stiff-necked after many rebukes will suddenly be destroyed—without remedy.* —Proverbs 29:1."

Dr. Martin replied, "Very good analysis, Dr. Carter. Dr. Carroll obviously believes that knowledge is key to success. This quality formed the foundation for his actions. The proverb you began with, '*I, wisdom, dwell together with prudence; I possess knowledge and discretion,*' (Proverbs 8:12) speaks to this prevailing admonition from King Solomon. Wisdom is related to knowledge. Dr. Carroll displays this proverb in his daily commitment to continual learning, and he goes above and beyond when he creates opportunities for his team to learn as well."

Dr. Martin said, "Dr. Barry Carroll is indeed an excellent example of a seeker of knowledge. Additionally, the analysis you provided of his work is stellar. This has been another productive learning time." Dr. Martin looked at his calendar and invited Katy to attend a session he was presenting on ethical leadership at the state administrators' conference in two weeks. He said, "This session will address the next quality: Wise leaders are ethical."

Katy quickly examined her calendar and found the proposed date to be open. "Yes, sir. Thank you for the kind invitation."

Dr. Martin said, "Good. Keep reading and look for proverbs related to ethics. And on your way out, please speak to Ms. Robertson about registering for the conference."

Katy replied, "Yes, sir. Thank you, Dr. Martin."

That night before retiring, Katy opened her journal to capture reflections from meeting with her mentor. Under the section, "Quality #2: Wise Leaders are Seekers of Knowledge," she looked at the list of proverbs that she had listed earlier:

1. *I, wisdom, dwell together with prudence; I possess knowledge and discretion.* —Proverbs 8:12
2. *Pay attention and listen to the sayings of the wise.* —Proverbs 22:17
3. *The prudent see danger and take refuge.* —Proverbs 27:12

4. *A man who remains stiff-necked after many rebukes will suddenly be destroyed—without remedy.* —Proverbs 29:1

Then, Katy posed the following for further deliberation:

- *What does it mean to be a seeker of knowledge?*
- *Compare "seeking knowledge" to national standards for educational leaders.*

Beneath the reflective questions, Katy wrote:
What does it mean to be a seeker of knowledge?

Being a seeker of knowledge means staying ahead or being proactive by continually seeking knowledge. Some leaders struggle with meeting deadlines and solving problems. The wise leader looks ahead and creates a vision with the team for how the school or district can be its best. The watchful leader is one who keeps a lookout for gaps or danger signs and plans a course of action to address these areas that need correction.

Being a seeker of knowledge also means continual learning—staying abreast of current research in order to lead the effort to improve student learning. Being a seeker of knowledge means staying on top of information—written, verbal, and nonverbal. The wise leader is not running behind; he/she meets all assigned deadlines and leads the way by being a seeker of knowledge.

In order to answer the second question, Katy reviewed the Council of Chief State School Officers Professional Standards for Educational Leaders (2015) and wrote in her journal:

The CCSSO Professional Standards for Educational Leaders addresses the need for continual learning, or seeking knowledge. In Standard 6, Professional Capacity of School Personnel, it states:

"Effective educational leaders develop the professional capacity and practice of school personnel to promote each student's academic success and well-being."

Through continual learning, Katy was developing her professional capacity and practice. Katy reviewed and adopted this definition of professional capacity from the Association of Supervision and Curriculum Development (ASCD): *Capacity-building professional development instills meaningful, ongoing learning in local professional communities.*

Pleased with her reflection, Katy closed her journal to seek a well-deserved night of blissful sleep.

COFFEE CHAT WITH GAIL MORGAN

The week before Katy was scheduled to attend the state administrators' conference, she had her monthly coffee chat with her friend and colleague, Gail Morgan. They had been friends and colleagues for years; they decided a couple of years ago to meet once a month to stretch each other's minds. They looked forward to their late afternoon coffee and intellectually stimulating conversation. They took turns defining the topic or book for each month's chat.

It was Katy's turn to pick the topic to discuss. She briefed Gail by email on leadership, according to Solomon, and introduced her to the seven qualities wise leaders possess. In particular, Katy wanted to discuss the qualities of seeking knowledge and embracing ethical leadership. This uplifting conversation would be an excellent precursor for the conference she would attend next week.

Katy enjoyed these shared moments of learning in a quiet, stress-free environment. They regularly met at Berkeley Bob's Coffee Shop. Gail was already there with a smile on her face when Katy arrived. Gail had the ability to brighten a room just by being in it. She was one of the most positive people Katy had ever known.

Katy admired Gail because of her friendly demeanor, her professionalism, and her work ethic. The two colleagues started teaching the same year in Washington County, and both landed in administrative posts. Gail's primary responsibility included planning the professional learning in the district and helping struggling teachers.

After they ordered their coffee, they skipped the small talk. Katy said, "There is a link between knowledge and ethical leadership, Gail. *Successful leaders seek knowledge, but they must carefully define the knowledge they wish to seek.* It is imperative that teachers and school leaders continually learn and understand that standards of excellence serve as guideposts in their continual improvement process."

Gail said, "Now more than ever before, school leadership requires unwavering commitment from school administrators and staff as they collectively strive to achieve excellence and equity for all students. The hours one spends engaged in professional learning can be hours that impact years in the lives of adults and students."

"That is so true," Katy replied.

Gail extracted a book from her bag and quickly turned to an earmarked page. Gail said, "In Thomas R. Hoerr's book, *The Art of School Leadership*, he writes, 'Good leaders change organizations; great leaders change people. People are the heart of any organization, particularly a school, and it is only through changing people—nurturing and challenging them, helping them grow and develop, creating a culture in which they all learn—that an organization can flourish. Leadership is about relationships.'"

Katy said, "Relationships are woven throughout Solomon's proverbs and can be seen in each of the seven qualities of successful leaders. For example, a leader can cast a vision, but if he doesn't have a relationship with others, who is there to hear him talk about the vision? And a leader must earn respect from others in order to achieve optimal effectiveness. In other words, successful interpersonal relationships must be developed before you can change people."

Gail said, "It's impossible to have effective leadership without cultivating relationships with those essential stakeholders investing in students and their success. The teaching profession requires its leaders to stretch and be stretched in many directions as faculty, staff, and students strive to meet the rigorous local, state, and national standards. Leadership is all about encouraging, invigorating, and enlightening the teachers and staff to create an environment of possibility for students."

Katy replied, "Standards, developed through professional organizations in concert with current research and legislation, help to define what to teach and how to behave in a civilized society. Leaders must be lifelong learners if they wish to lead others."

Gail said, "The principal's role is in a constant state of change. It is absolutely critical to be proactive and stay one, two, or three steps ahead. What better place to take this journey than in the company of leading thinkers in education? Look at this graphic for our summer conference. It speaks to this need."

Katy looked at the attractive flyer. It posed the following questions:

As you consider your present situation do you desire to:

- Gain new insight into best practices to implement immediately in your school?
- Discover innovative initiatives happening in our state, nation, and world?
- Renew a sense of optimism about the opportunities available for students?
- Expand your personal and/or professional growth?
- Learn the most current skills and strategies to meet the ever-changing needs of schools?
- Meet new colleagues and expand your professional network with administrators across our state?
- Transform your thinking about effective leadership practices to meet your current challenges?
- Learn about current state department of education updates?
- Keep up-to-date with your instructional leadership certification?
- Be energized, refreshed, and motivated to meet the challenges and demands of school leadership?

All of this and so much more is readily available when we step out and expand our network to include leaders outside our building, district, state, or even nation. There is always much to be learned from others.

The flyer then listed the pertinent information about the conference: location, registration, speakers, and professional standards related to the learning opportunities. Katy said, "This flyer for your conference is outstanding, Gail. This professional learning event will be stellar." Bob placed two cups of café au lait on the table in front of each lady.

Gail said, "In your email, you mentioned that successful leaders possess vision, according to Solomon. This made me think about an article I read in Learning Forward's journal *The Learning Professional*. It reported on the Wallace Foundation's extensive research on things effective principals do that ripple through classrooms and boost learning, especially in failing schools." Gail extracted the printed copy of the article from her bag, and placed it on the table. She continued, "The research lists five practices that seem central to effective school leadership."

Katy read the list:

1. Shaping a vision of academic success for all students, one based on high standards;
2. Creating a climate hospitable to education in order that safety, a cooperative spirit, and other foundations of fruitful interaction prevail;
3. Cultivating leadership in others so that teachers and other adults assume their part in realizing their school visions;
4. Improving instruction to enable teachers to teach at their best and students to learn at their utmost; and
5. Managing people, data, and processes to foster school improvement.

Katy said, "Cultivating leadership and improving instruction work together for continuous school improvement. How do school administrators cultivate leadership and improve instruction? They do so by being lifelong learners."

Gail nodded her head in agreement and said, "Most people, regardless of their role in life, would agree they desire to be successful, but far too many are unwilling to 'sharpen the saw' and do the work.

"Stephen Covey, in his popular book, *The 7 Habits of Highly Effective People*, wrote about 'sharpening the saw.' He used the analogy to encourage leaders to preserve and enhance the greatest asset they have—themselves. The woodcutter used in Covey's analogy was continually frustrated with the inefficiency of his dull blade, yet he never took time to stop and sharpen it.

"The same is true with professional learning. If leaders do not make time to break away and sharpen the saw, share ideas, and consider other perspectives, then they limit not only their growth opportunities, but also the opportunity to lead new thinking and improve options for their students. John Wooden, Hall of Fame basketball coach, said, 'It's what you learn after you know it all that counts.'"

Gail said, "Take a look at this comment from a highly successful principal who is continually seeking knowledge." Gail laid the evaluation sheet on the table for Katy to read:

I LOVE the Certified Instructional Leadership program because it:

1. Holds me accountable as a leader,
2. Forces me to grow as a leader,
3. Gives me a group of people who are going through what I am going through,
4. Has purpose and value to actually assist a principal in his/her school,
5. Is EXACTLY what I needed to take my school and my leadership to the next level, and
6. Represents what a principal or leader can do NOW, this year, to improve!

Katy said, "This principal is a positive, enthusiastic leader, it seems. I can tell just by reading the comments. Didn't you write a blog about the importance of professional learning recently?"

Gail said, "Yes, that is correct." Gail handed a printed copy of the blog to Katy and said, "The state conference next week should be outstanding. Would you be kind enough to share the information from Dr. Martin's presentation with your coffee chat colleague?"

Katy smiled and said, "Yes, absolutely." The colleagues said their goodbyes. They both were busy people, but they made it a priority to connect with one another. They learned from each other each time they had a coffee chat. Katy thought of Solomon's proverb, "As iron sharpens iron, so one man sharpens another."

GAIL'S BLOG

That night, like all nights, Katy read. Tonight she read Gail's blog. Curled up on the couch with her grandmother's quilt around her, she read:

The Power of Professional Learning, by Gail Morgan

As Bill Nye the Science Guy says, "Everyone you will ever meet knows something that you don't. Respect their knowledge and learn from them. It will bring out the best in all of you." Do your stakeholders view you as a leader of learning? Are your decisions based on what's right for all students?

In "Leaders of Learning" by Richard DuFour and Robert Marzano, a profound thought is posed: "Don't ask if you are leading; you are. Don't ask if you are making a difference; you are. The question is, What kind of leader will you be and what kind of difference will you make?" Effective principal leadership can transform a culture of isolation into a culture of collaboration. DuFour and Marzano note that "principals do indeed make a difference in student learning, and the most powerful strategy for having a positive impact on that learning is to facilitate the learning of the educators who serve those students through the professional learning community process."

Principals strive continuously to grow their professional learning communities (PLCs). It cannot be accomplished overnight and is often a slow and steady process. It is essential that administrators put their knowledge into practice and consider the following:

- How can they help their fellow educators grow professionally?
- Is the principal modeling what it's like to be a learner?
- Does the principal have a vision for the many ways that teaching and learning are changing?
- How can the principal lead his staff to meet countless, diverse student needs?
- Is the school providing more technology opportunities for students to make its use seamless in day-to-day teaching and learning?
- How can their school/district tap into the power of social media for collaboration and communication?

In building effective PLCs there are stages of development, and it takes the continual practice and perseverance of each member to reach the ultimate goal. Noted author of *The Five Dysfunctions of a Team: A Leadership Fable*, Patrick Lencioni, says it best: "If you could get all the people in an organization rowing in the same direction, you could dominate any industry, in any market, against any competition, at any time." It's a constant work in progress but the ultimate reward, improved student achievement, is worth every effort.

School and district leaders consistently function in expansion mode to lead productive organizations. Douglas Reeves, author of *The Learning Leader*, reminds us that "Many people live their lives aspiring to make a difference and to live a life that matters. There need be no such uncertainty in the life of an educator or school leaders. Every decision we make, from daily interactions with students to the most constitutional policy at every level of government, will influence leadership and learning."

Great leaders constantly expand their thinking to influence others to provide the best opportunities for students. All leaders will leave a legacy for our students, staff, and schools. What will be your legacy?

George Bernard Shaw wrote: "This is the true joy in life, the being used for a purpose recognized by yourself as a mighty one; the being a force of nature instead of a feverish, selfish little clod of ailments and grievances complaining that the world will not devote itself to making you happy. I am of the opinion that my life belongs to the whole community, and as long as I live it is my privilege to do for it whatever I can. I want to be thoroughly used up when I die, for the harder I work the more I live. I rejoice in life for its own sake; life is no 'brief candle' to me. It is a sort of splendid torch which I have got hold of for the moment, and I want to make it burn as brightly as possible before handing it on to future generations."

The splendid torch which we hold for the moment . . . to make it burn as brightly as possible before handing it on to future generations . . .

Stroll down the winding path to the end of your professional journey . . . that last line that you write. What do you hope to accomplish? The lines we are currently writing will one day be our last. Will we be known as leaders that do everything possible within our scope of influence to ensure students are prepared for a successful future? Will our last line support that we valued professional learning and made it a priority to provide best practices for our students? Certainly our students, our future, are worth every effort.

Katy was inspired by Gail's blog entry. Professional learning was powerful, indeed. Katy was a lifelong learner. She related to every word that Gail wrote. She went to sleep thinking about how the professional books she read in the past related to Solomon's timeless, wise admonitions.

Chapter Three

Quality #3: Wise Leaders Are Ethical

By justice a king gives a country stability. —Proverbs 29:4

STATE CONFERENCE

It was dark at 5:30 a.m. And so it was that Katy Elle was driving in the early morning hours to the state capitol for the state administrators' conference. This day promised to provide a new experience for this enthusiastic school leader.

Katy made the proper arrangements for her professional learning opportunity. She connected with Dr. Martin's secretary for registration details. She completed the professional leave form, and added the event to her digital calendar so that the school secretary and assistant principals could view her schedule in their shared calendar. When she was out of the building she wanted her team to know where she was and what she would be doing.

The day before she left, Katy sent an email to her team at Independence High School:

> Subject: Out of Building for Professional Leave—KC
> Dear IHS Colleagues,
> I will be attending the state administrators' conference on Wednesday and Thursday of this week. Attending this conference aligns with my professional development plan goal #1: to provide ethical leadership in my service as principal at Independence High School.
> This goal is in concert with the Professional Standards for Educational Leaders (2015), Standard #2: "Effective educational leaders act ethically and according to professional norms to promote EACH student's academic success and well-being. Effective leaders:

a. Act ethically and professionally in personal conduct, relationships with others, decision-making, stewardship of the school's resources, and all aspects of school leadership.
b. Act according to and promote the professional norms of integrity, fairness, transparency, trust, collaboration, perseverance, learning, and continuous improvement.
c. Place children at the center of education and accept responsibility for each student's academic success and well-being.
d. Safeguard and promote the values of democracy, individual freedom and responsibility, equity, social justice, community, and diversity.
e. Lead with interpersonal and communication skill, social–emotional insight, and understanding of all students' and staff members' backgrounds and cultures.
f. Provide moral direction for the school and promote ethical and professional behavior among faculty and staff."

Assistant Principal Smith will be the principal in charge during my leave. In particular, I look forward to hearing Superintendent Martin's presentation on ethical leadership at the conference. I will share what I learn with you at our scheduled leadership team meeting next month. Make it a great week!
—Katy

Katy stopped to get a cup of coffee at 7:00 a.m. She still had another hour to drive until she reached her destination. During her travel, she listened to classical music. She enjoyed watching the darkness disappear as the sun revealed itself from the east in a glorious display of orange and yellow.

Dr. Carter arrived at the conference center at 8:15 a.m. She was happy to be early, as it made her feel relaxed and confident. She parked her car and went inside to find the registration area. After Katy received her conference packet, she put her name tag on and went to find a seat close to the front. She planned to catch up on emails until the program began.

At 8:55 a.m. the ballroom was packed with school and district leaders from across the state. There must have been at least four hundred educational leaders attending the conference. Katy felt the energy in the room and the excitement of being with like-minded individuals.

The executive director of the superintendents' professional association welcomed the attendees promptly at 9:00 a.m., and asked a superintendent to come forward to lead the invocation. Then, the executive director of the principals' association came to the podium. He said, "Good morning. Why should you make it a priority to be a member of your professional organizations? There are three reasons to do so.

1. Standards are developed from such organizations, and these standards serve as guideposts for school leaders.

2. Interpersonal relationships are forged that provide emotional and professional support.
3. Furthermore, the legislative side cannot be ignored. How could any school leader stay abreast of current events in the legislature without guidance such as that which is provided from professional organizations?

"The mission of most school leader organizations focuses on the coordination and facilitation of resources of all members for the advancement of education, the school leader profession, and individual needs, personally and professionally. Usually, school leader associations provide valuable services supporting their mission relating to professional development, networking opportunities, communications, legislative representation/advocacy, legal services, and various awards and recognition programs.

"Why join a professional association? Kelly A. Cherwin, director of editorial strategy at HigherEdJobs, wrote, 'If you are interested in furthering your career, joining a professional association is a good start. An association is a synergistic group, meaning that the effect of a collection of people is greater than just one person.' She also explains why becoming part of a synergistic group can help further your career goals. Ms. Cherwin also shared that 'enhancing your network' is a tremendous benefit of joining an association.

"She stated that 'For most people, creating professional relationships is important, and joining a group allows you to have a sense of security and trust. From this, you are able to support and help one another in reaching your professional goals. Associations sponsor numerous events throughout the year that allow you to connect with your peers. You can share ideas, ask for advice, volunteer to be a speaker, or become a member of a committee.

"Since most associations have national or local conferences, you can participate and have the opportunity to learn about breaking news in your career, learn *best practices* or new ideas, hear about key achievers in your field and also meet and brainstorm with others who are also looking to share and learn new information. Another benefit of enhancing your network is that you may find a mentor to help you with your professional needs or you may be in a position to become a mentor to someone else. Giving back can be the greatest reward and benefit'" (Cherwin 2010).

"Why else should you join a professional association? Earl Leonard, past president of our organization and retired elementary principal at West Morgan Elementary, said that 'The connections you can make with other administrators seem endless. You can call any of the members to ask for advice or help on an issue and all would be willing to help in any way possible.'"

"As we travel through the process of professional change, principals should remember that change takes time and the professional organization is here to give support and provide networking opportunities and quality professional learning activities and events," shared Dr. Lydia Davenport, past president of the state's Association of Elementary School Administrators.

The executive director, Dr. Earl Franks, continued, "Associations advocate, through the voices of united members, to protect the unique and critical role of school leaders, promote members' vision for education reform, and preserve the profession through high-quality professional learning and other member service opportunities. The American Society of Association Executives (ASAE) is the essential organization for association management, representing both organizations and individual association professionals.

"ASAE states that, 'associations have the power to transform society for the better. Our passion is to help association professionals achieve previously unimaginable levels of performance. We do this by nurturing a community of smart, creative, and interesting people: our members.' Most associations mirror the beliefs and practices outlined by ASAE:

- Build knowledge. Associations are a definitive source for ideas, tools, and resources for the association profession.
- Enable learning. Associations provide exceptional learning experiences that enable their members to consistently produce superior results.
- Foster community. Associations engage professionals and industry partners in a diverse, global, welcoming community.
- Engage in advocacy. Associations' advocacy and communications efforts enhance recognition for the profession and result in a positive legislative and regulatory climate for the members they serve.

"In closing, you are to be commended for being here today. Your attendance at this conference reveals that you are making it a high priority to participate in your professional organization. Standards are developed from professional organizations such as this one, and these standards serve as guideposts for school leaders. Through your participation, you will forge interpersonal relationships that will provide emotional and professional support. And you will be aware of the current events in the legislature through the advocacy and involvement of our organization."

Dr. Franks told the group that throughout his career he improved his professional practice because he embraced identified standards and sought continual improvement through learning, networking with others, and knowledge and advocacy of changing legislation. When he concluded, everyone applauded. Katy clearly saw the benefits of learning corporately and individually. But until now, she had not made it a priority to attend state meetings. Katy was motivated to make this a necessity in the future.

DR. MARTIN'S PRESENTATION

After a brief introduction, Dr. Martin came to the podium. His presentation, *Ethical Leadership in Our Schools*, was next. Katy was impressed. She did not realize that her mentor and superintendent was the keynote speaker for this state conference. Dr. Martin was a respected educational leader not only in his community, but at the state level as well.

Ronnie Martin quickly walked to the podium and paused for approximately five seconds. It was so quiet in the ballroom. Then he said, "Solomon, the son of David, the king of Israel, the wisest and richest king that ever lived, wrote proverbs 'for gaining wisdom and instruction; for understanding words of insight; for receiving instruction in prudent behavior, *doing what is right and just and fair*' (Proverbs 1:1-3). He said, 'By justice a king gives a country stability' (Proverbs 29:4).

"Ethical leaders do what is right and just and fair. Are you an ethical leader? What is ethics? According to Webster's definition, ethics is a branch of philosophy that deals with what is morally right or wrong. We have rules of behavior based on these ideas in two forms:

1. These rules are taught to students each day in the form of character education.
2. The rules for professional behavior are delineated in a code of ethics.

"It is a state mandate to have ten minutes of a character education per day for all K–12 students. In Paul Tough's book *How Children Succeed*, he states that the most important qualities related to student success have to do with character. These skills include perseverance, curiosity, conscientiousness, optimism, and self-control.

"Remember Andy Griffith? In his popular television show, he taught us character lessons in each episode. Andy knew how to solve problems and he taught us, by example, to do the right thing. How did teachers know what was the 'right thing' to do in the early days?" Dr. Martin displayed a slide with a list of "teacher rules" from 1872. He said, "Look at this list of 'teacher rules' from 1872:

1. Will fill lamps, trim wicks, and clean chimneys.
2. Each morning teacher will bring bucket of water and a scuttle of coal for the day's session.
3. Make your pens carefully. You may whittle nibs to the individual taste of the pupils.
4. Men teachers may take one evening each week for courting purposes or two evenings a week if they attend church regularly.

5. After ten hours in school the teachers may spend the remaining time reading the Bible or any other good book.
6. Women teachers who marry or engage in unseemly conduct will be dismissed.
7. Every teacher should lay aside for each pay day a goodly sum of his earnings for his benefit during his declining years so that he will not become a burden on society.
8. Any teacher who smokes, uses liquor in any form, frequents pool or public halls, or gets shaved in a barber shop will give good reason to suspect his worth, intention, integrity, and honesty.
9. The teacher who performs his labor faithfully and without fault for five years will be given an increase of $0.25 per week in his pay, providing the board of education approves.

"Here are rules for teachers from 1915:
Rules for Teachers—1915

1. You will not marry during the term of your contract.
2. You are not to keep company with men.
3. You must be home between the hours of 8:00 p.m. and 6:00 a.m. unless at a school function.
4. You may not loiter downtown in any of the ice cream stores.
5. You may not travel beyond the city limits unless you have the permission of the chairman of the school board.
6. You may not ride in carriages or automobiles with any man except your father or brother.
7. You may not smoke cigarettes.
8. You may not dress in bright colors.
9. You may under no circumstances dye your hair.
10. You must wear at least two petticoats.
11. Your dresses may not be any shorter than two inches above the ankles.
12. To keep the classroom neat and clean you must sweep the floor once a day, scrub the floor with hot soapy water once a week, clean the blackboards once a day and start the fire at 7:00 a.m. to have the school warm by 8:00 a.m. when the scholars arrive.

"Teachers certainly had a lot of rules back then. The truth is all professions have rules, standards, or a code of ethics. For example, the American Medical Association, the American Bar Association, the American Institute of CPAs, the National Society of Professional Engineers, the American Institute of Architects, and the National Association of Evangelicals have codes of ethics. The United States Office of Government Ethics also has a code of ethics. And the education profession has a code of ethics as well.

"The National Education Association has a code of ethics for educators, and the Council of Chief State School Officers, in collaboration with the National Policy Board for Educational Administration, provides a code of ethics called the Professional Standards for Educational Leaders." Dr. Martin advanced to the next slide to share the ten standards:

Professional Standards for Educational Leaders (2015)
Standard 1. Mission, Vision, and Core Values
Standard 2. Ethics and Professional Norms
Standard 3. Equity and Cultural Responsiveness
Standard 4. Curriculum, Instruction, and Assessment
Standard 5. Community of Care and Support for Students
Standard 6. Professional Capacity of School Personnel
Standard 7. Professional Community for Teachers and Staff
Standard 8. Meaningful Engagement of Families and Community
Standard 9. Operations and Management
Standard 10. School Improvement

"Look at Standard 2: Ethics and Professional Norms. It states: 'Effective educational leaders act ethically and according to professional norms to promote *each* student's academic success and well-being.'"

Katy remembered reviewing this standard during her time of reflection and completion of professional leave paperwork. *These standards are student-centered*, she thought.

"Most states have their own code of ethics for educators as well. And how is adherence to these codes monitored? Usually, an ethics commission oversees violations of an ethical nature. Additionally, school districts have their own policies related to standards of behavior for educators. Some refer to the state code of ethics when expressing expectations for employees' job performance.

"The National Education Association (NEA) has a Code of Ethics of the Education Profession. It includes a preamble that states":

The National Education Association believes that the education profession consists of one education workforce serving the needs of all students, and that the term "educator" includes education support professionals.

The educator, believing in the worth and dignity of each human being, recognizes the supreme importance of the pursuit of truth, devotion to excellence, and the nurture of the democratic principles. Essential to these goals is the protection of freedom to learn and to teach and the guarantee of equal educational opportunity for all. The educator accepts the responsibility to adhere to the highest ethical standards.

The educator recognizes the magnitude of the responsibility inherent in the teaching process. The desire for the respect and confidence of one's colleagues, of students, of parents, and of the members of the community provides the incentive to attain and maintain the highest possible degree of ethical conduct. The "Code of Ethics of the Education Profession" indicates the aspiration of all educators and provides standards by which to judge conduct.

"The NEA 'Code of Ethics' includes a Commitment to the Student in Principle I:

PRINCIPLE I
COMMITMENT TO THE STUDENT
The educator strives to help each student realize his or her potential as a worthy and effective member of society. The educator therefore works to stimulate the spirit of inquiry, the acquisition of knowledge and understanding, and the thoughtful formulation of worthy goals.

In fulfillment of the obligation to the student, the educator—

1. Shall not unreasonably restrain the student from independent action in the pursuit of learning.
2. Shall not unreasonably deny the student's access to varying points of view.
3. Shall not deliberately suppress or distort subject matter relevant to the student's progress.
4. Shall make reasonable effort to protect the student from conditions harmful to learning or to health and safety.
5. Shall not intentionally expose the student to embarrassment or disparagement.
6. Shall not on the basis of race, color, creed, sex, national origin, marital status, political or religious beliefs, family, social or cultural background, or sexual orientation, unfairly—

    a. exclude any student from participation in any program
    b. deny benefits to any student
    c. grant any advantage to any student

7. Shall not use professional relationships with students for private advantage.
8. Shall not disclose information about students obtained in the course of professional service unless disclosure serves a compelling professional purpose or is required by law.

"As you can see, our society has high expectations for those in the teaching profession. The Apostle James said, 'Don't be in any rush to become a teacher, my friends. Teaching is highly responsible work. Teachers are held to the strictest standards' (James 3:1). Let's look at Principle II, Commitment to the Profession":

PRINCIPLE II
COMMITMENT TO THE PROFESSION
The education profession is vested by the public with a trust and responsibility requiring the highest ideals of professional service.

In the belief that the quality of the services of the education profession directly influences the nation and its citizens, the educator shall exert every effort to raise professional standards, to promote a climate that encourages the exercise of professional judgment, to achieve conditions that attract persons worthy of trust to careers in education, and to assist in preventing the practice of the profession by unqualified persons.

In fulfillment of the obligation to the profession, the educator—

1. Shall not in an application for a professional position deliberately make a false statement or fail to disclose a material fact related to competency and qualifications.
2. Shall not misrepresent his or her professional qualifications.
3. Shall not assist any entry into the profession of a person known to be unqualified in respect to character, education, or other relevant attribute.
4. Shall not knowingly make a false statement concerning the qualifications of a candidate for a professional position.
5. Shall not assist a noneducator in the unauthorized practice of teaching.
6. Shall not disclose information about colleagues obtained in the course of professional service unless disclosure serves a compelling professional purpose or is required by law.
7. Shall not knowingly make false or malicious statements about a colleague.
8. Shall not accept any gratuity, gift, or favor that might impair or appear to influence professional decisions or action.

Adopted by the NEA 1975 Representative Assembly

"Turn to your colleague and talk about your district's code of ethics or board policy related to ethics or standards for behavior. Compare it to the NEA 'Code of Ethics.'"

After a few minutes, Dr. Martin said, "Let's look at the state's Educator Code of Ethics. It includes nine standards":

1. Professional Conduct
2. Trustworthiness
3. Unlawful Acts
4. Teacher/Student Relationship
5. Alcohol, Drug, and Tobacco Use or Possession
6. Public Funds and Property
7. Remunerative Conduct
8. Maintenance of Confidentiality
9. Abandonment of Contract

"It is interesting to note that educators are required to report a breach of one or more of the standards. Let's look at number six, Principle I of the NEA 'Code of Ethics'":

> 6. Shall not on the basis of race, color, creed, sex, national origin, marital status, political or religious beliefs, family, social or cultural background, or sexual orientation, unfairly—
>
>   a. exclude any student from participation in any program
>   b. deny benefits to any student
>   c. grant any advantage to any student

King Solomon spoke to fairness in his proverbs. He said,

- To show partiality is not good. —Proverbs 28:21
- Those who give to the poor will lack nothing, but those who close their eyes to them receive many curses. —Proverbs 28:27
- If a king judges the poor with fairness, his throne will be established forever. —Proverbs 29:14

"Students must be treated fairly. School leaders must seek to exemplify qualities they wish to instill in their students such as honesty, perseverance, and trustworthiness. They must display professional conduct, avoid unlawful acts, and avoid any hint of an inappropriate relationship with students or staff. They must exhibit self-control in all areas of their life, personally and professionally. They must be careful in handling public funds.

"School leaders must speak up for those who cannot speak for themselves. They must represent the disabled, the fatherless or motherless, and the poor. And, school leaders must be bold about it. Solomon said, 'The wicked flee though no one pursues, but the righteous are as bold as a lion' (Proverbs 28:1).

"Principals and superintendents must demand that teachers provide instruction based on the latest teaching methods. And, they must ensure that instruction is based on standards determined by our state and district." Dr. Martin advanced to the next slide. It was a photo of a teacher's tombstone.

He continued, "Carved in the tombstone of Ms. Nancy Elizabeth Monroe, it stated, 'FAITHFUL TO HER TRUST EVEN UNTIL DEATH.'" Dr. Martin paused to give the leaders an opportunity to reflect. Then he said, "What will you be remembered for after you are gone? What will others say about you? Will you be remembered as an ethical leader?" Dr. Martin walked off the stage as the educational leaders applauded.

After Dr. Martin's presentation, there was a thirty-minute break. During this time, Katy was able to connect with her mentor to tell him how much she enjoyed his presentation. Then she attended other sessions during the conference related to technology, instruction, human resources, finances, and leadership.

CONVERSATION WITH SENATOR BUSSMAN

The conference ended the next day after lunch. Katy decided to enjoy a cup of coffee in the hotel coffee shop before she started the drive home. Katy placed her order and sat down at a small table to review her notes while she drank her coffee. She was lost in thought about the ethical leadership presentation Dr. Martin provided when Senator Paul Bussman (Alabama) walked over to Katy and said, "Afternoon, Dr. Carter."

Katy stood up and extended her hand as she said, "Senator, it is so nice to see you."

Paul said, "It looks like you are studying."

Katy quickly summarized her study on the wise proverbs from Solomon, directed by her mentor, Dr. Martin. The senator shared that he became an elected leader because of a truth he discovered in the Bible years ago. He said, "In Deuteronomy 15:11, it states: 'For there will never cease to be poor in the land. Therefore I command you, you shall open wide your hand to your brother, to the needy and to the poor, in your land'" (New American Standard Bible).

Katy said, "How interesting. There is a proverb related to defending the rights of the poor and needy as well." Katy opened her journal to find the proverb. She said, "Here it is. In Proverbs 31:8–9, Solomon wrote, 'Speak up for those who cannot speak for themselves, for the rights of all who are destitute. Speak up and judge fairly; defend the rights of the poor and needy.'"

Senator Bussman replied, "As a child, raised primarily by a divorced mother on a very limited income, it would have been very easy for the third child of five to go unnoticed and 'slip through the cracks' of the world. Fortunately, that was not the case, because many people chose to get involved." Senator Bussman shared that he had a mother who loved him very much, cared for him, and made him understand that even though they were limited financially, there were people less fortunate than them that needed their help. His mother's service to others was very obvious.

Katy asked, "Did you have a mentor?"

Paul told Katy that one man became a very influential father figure for him. His name was Dr. Jack Vogel, and Paul called him "Dr. Jack." This very successful dentist willingly got involved in Paul's life and quietly taught him how to act as a man. He taught him to shake hands firmly, to hold the doors for women, and to do a hard day's work. Dr. Jack would take Paul to Alabama football games. Instead of possibly enjoying the game more without a young teenager, he chose to bring Paul along. He clearly understood the importance of mentoring.

During Paul's senior year in dental school, in 1982, Dr. Jack invited him to join his dental practice. The first day Dr. Bussman started in his practice, Dr. Jack called him into his office and told him that he was very fortunate. He reminded Paul of all the people that helped him over the last twenty-plus years. He told Paul that it was now his time to serve and give back to others. Dr. Jack instilled in the senator the need to be aware of those that could fall through the cracks and help them when possible.

They practiced together for seven wonderful years, Senator Bussman shared. During that period he truly began to understand the importance of service and taking care of those that are less fortunate. He watched Dr. Jack's example of giving thousands of dollars in free dental care, without saying a word. He watched Dr. Jack willingly lead and serve in many areas of the community. Since that time, Paul said he tried to follow that great example.

Katy replied, "Senator, didn't you help to start Volunteers in Public Schools, a mentoring program for at-risk children in our local schools? Also, weren't you involved in the group that started the Good Samaritan Health Clinic, a medical, dental, and optical program for those hardworking people that had no health insurance?"

Senator Bussman said, "Yes."

Katy replied, "And now, as a member of the state senate, you continue to be a vocal supporter of foster children and those least able to help themselves."

The senator said, "As these instrumental people pass away, all leaders must assume the responsibility to carry the torch for a new generation."

Katy said, "Thank you for sharing this story. It creates an awareness of the tremendous responsibility citizens and leaders have to be there for others in need. Dr. Jack's willingness to mentor you stands as a reminder that all leaders need to notice people coming behind them." Katy knew she planned to become a mentor one day because of the example provided by Dr. Martin. Senator Bussman and Katy said their farewells. He told Katy, "Take care of all kids, Dr. Carter." Katy promised him that she would do so.

Before Katy left the coffee shop, she posed questions for reflection in her journal related to ethical leadership.

QUESTIONS FOR REFLECTION:
Quality #3—Wise Leaders Are Ethical

1. *Identify a leader who stands up for the poor and needy.*
2. *How does this person represent those who cannot represent themselves?*

3. *Am I am impartial leader? Do I show favoritism to students, friends, or people of influence? Do I spend more time in one teacher's classroom or school or office than another's?*
4. *How do Solomon's proverbs relate to professional educational leadership standards in my state or at the national level?*

It was time for Katy to get on the road to make it home before dark. She closed her journal, collected her things, and headed home to see Daniel.

Chapter Four

Quality #4: Wise Leaders Are Humble

When pride comes, then comes disgrace, but with humility comes wisdom.
—Proverbs 11:2

The next morning Katy was back at school at 7:00 a.m., standing in the commons area to greet students as they started their day. Students, team members, and parents knew where to locate the principal each morning. Katy listened. She smiled. She noticed her students and called them by name when they approached her.

A couple of the student council officers came up to Katy and said, "Is the spaghetti supper still at your home Saturday night, Dr. Carter?"

Katy replied, "Yes. It will be a relaxed, fun evening to celebrate your service as leaders at Independence High School." Katy and Daniel were looking forward to the evening and she couldn't wait to hear their ideas about ways to improve their school. Her beautiful students beamed as they talked to their principal. The students said good-bye and hurried off to see friends and get to their first period class.

Seeing the students reminded Katy that she needed to pick up the paperweights she ordered. She planned to present them to the student council officers Saturday night. Mr. Palys, the owner of the local trophy shop, saved Carrara marble remnants for Katy. A brass plate would be affixed to the top of each of the marble remnants, engraved with the name of the student and school, the office the student held, and the school year. She was anxious to see the special gifts, and even more anxious to give them to her precious students as a little memento of their honored leadership position at IHS.

The last bell rang, signifying it was time for class to begin. Katy did a quick walk-through of the facility and returned to her office. She retrieved her messages and reviewed her calendar for the day. Then, Katy picked up her laptop and headed to the library to respond to email and read. When she finished reading emails, Katy planned to read from the book that was selected by the leadership team. It was about student engagement, and it was recommended reading in the school-wide professional learning community (PLC).

The first email Katy read was from her mentor, in response to the email she sent him to thank him for the opportunity to attend the state administrators' conference. It was a valuable learning experience. He replied:

Dr. Carter,

It is fantastic that you could attend the conference, and that you found it to be beneficial in your quest to seek knowledge. It is a favorite conference for many leaders. A tremendous amount of information is shared at this professional meeting.

So far, in our study of Solomon's proverbs, you learned about the first three qualities that wise leaders possess:

1. *vision,*
2. *knowledge, and*
3. *ethics.*

Now it is time to learn about the fourth quality—humility. A favorite proverb related to humility comes from Proverbs 11:2:

"When pride comes, then comes disgrace, but with humility comes wisdom."

Can you find any other proverbs that speak to the quality of humility? Your next assignment is to identify a leader that personifies this important quality, and arrange a meeting with this person.

Thank You,

R.M.

This was an easy assignment. Katy immediately identified the humble servant leader in her school. It was Jan Ingram, the PTA president. A PTA board meeting was scheduled for the next week. Katy would invite the superintendent to attend this meeting. Katy sent a calendar invitation to Dr. Martin, and he confirmed his attendance.

Katy continued to think about humility and remembered a comment she once read about servant leadership or humility from Jeremy Oden, public service commissioner. When Katy returned to her office, she found the comment in a saved newspaper article. Commissioner Oden said,

When an individual is placed in a leadership position, especially by his or her peers, the power is not in the position but rather the expression of humility and love for others.

When these two important ingredients, humility and love, are evident, then the art of servant leadership is developed. Serving others will create more power in any individual than any position can. When a leader possesses the power of a servant, he sees beyond the surface into the depths of why. This is especially applicable to a leader in seeing the needs of children and the poor. A servant leader will always ask why and in doing so create the advocate needed to lead for all.

Jan Ingram expressed humility and love for others. She was the perfect example of Solomon's humility.

JAN INGRAM

Before the PTA board meeting, President Ingram scheduled a time to review the agenda with Katy. Their planning meetings were always uplifting and helpful, and this time was no different. Katy sat at the conference table with Jan as they looked over her draft agenda.

The agenda included a reminder that Teacher Appreciation Week was approaching. Jan wanted it to be extra special for their dedicated faculty. Jan also wanted to update the PTA bylaws, and plan for the Spring Arts Alive event, where student artwork would be displayed. After reviewing other business items, the president confirmed the upcoming PTA board meeting date and location before she sent an email reminder to board members.

A GIFT OF ENCOURAGEMENT AND LOVE

On the morning of the board meeting, Katy was scheduled to conduct classroom observations. She captured the time for evaluations on her calendar weeks in advance. Otherwise, "some urgent matter" in the office would prevent her from doing so. While Katy was observing instruction, Jan Ingram came to her office with a large basket and a stepladder.

Secretly, she arranged a time with Cynthia Perkins, the school secretary, to sneak into the principal's office to decorate it while Katy was observing classes. Jan's large, colorful basket, woven with paper from recycled magazines, contained command strips, thumb tacks, tape, cotton kite string, small clothespins, notes for Dr. Carter from students, six-inch letters—made from red, white and blue construction paper—and a string of clear Christmas tree lights. The PTA president quickly started decorating the principal's office.

On the wall across from Katy's desk, Jan mounted the kite string from one end of the wall to the other. Cynthia came in to check on Jan and helped her as much as she could. When they finished their work, four parallel strings hung loosely on the wall. In the middle of the four strings, the ladies affixed colorful letters to the wall with tape. The letters spelled out:

WE LOVE YOU, DR. CARTER!

Then, they attached the students' letters to the strings with clothespins. These treasured letters came from students who voluntarily wrote notes to their principal during English class. The notes were written on simple ruled note-book paper. Jan Ingram asked the English department team leader for assistance in this project; she was happy to offer this special opportunity to students. When the ladies completed their task, they were pleased with the outcome. The sea of letters covered the wall, and the Christmas lights softly illuminated the top row of letters. A simple red rose in a bud vase was left on the principal's desk as a reminder of the PTA's support.

When Dr. Carter returned to her office, she was greeted with the heart-warming, thoughtful display of affection. The office light was turned off, and the twinkling lights softly showcased the precious display. Katy was speech-less. Cynthia and other staff members joined her in the principal's office to express amazement and admiration for the creative display of encouragement and love. They walked from letter to letter as if they were in a fine museum admiring priceless treasures. Indeed, they were. Katy's favorite letter read,

Dr. Carter,
You are the heart of our school.
Love,
Lauren

THE PTA BOARD MEETING

Before Jan Ingram filled Katy's office with love, she prepared the conference room for the PTA board meeting. She expected approximately fourteen parents to attend the meeting, and she made sure that there were fourteen chairs surrounding the long conference table. Two extra chairs were against the wall in case they were needed. A professional agenda was placed at each board member's place along with the minutes from the previous meeting; perpendicular to the agenda, a red ink pen was found. The phrase, *You make a difference!* was printed on the pen. At the top of the agenda, the time was stated: *Noon – 1:00 p.m.*

Two large crock-pots, filled with delicious, hot chili, were on the table at the back of the conference room along with paper plates and bowls, spoons and napkins. Jan brought saltine crackers, Mexican cornbread, grated ched-dar cheese, and sour cream. She also brought tortilla chips and salsa. Jan made brownies, fudge, and lemon squares for dessert. She also had tea and water ready to be poured into the cups already filled with ice. And fresh daisies filled a wide mouth Mason jar, and brought beauty from the outside into the conference room.

It was 11:45 a.m. when Dr. Martin arrived for the PTA board meeting. Katy welcomed him in the front office lobby. Cynthia said, "Dr. Martin, please go back to Dr. Carter's office and see the sweet notes from students."

He said, "Certainly. That sounds interesting." Katy felt a little embarrassed about the display he would soon see in her office, but she went with Dr. Martin, and she enjoyed looking at the letters with her superintendent. While reading the wonderful notes, Dr. Martin exclaimed, "What an absolutely fantastic idea! You are a lucky principal, Dr. Carter, to work in this positive, caring atmosphere."

Katy quickly said, "Yes, sir, Dr. Martin, it is an honor to serve as the principal of Independence High School. It is an excellent school that is filled with dedicated leaders and sweet students. We have a wonderful PTA, too. You are about to observe a great servant leader named Jan Ingram. She is our PTA president, and she exemplifies the fourth quality of leadership, according to Solomon: humility."

Dr. Martin asked, "Did she coordinate this letter-writing effort?"

Katy replied, "Yes, she did. Jan is the most thoughtful lady."

Katy and Dr. Martin continued talking as they walked to the conference room. They were attending the PTA board meeting to observe the humble leadership of Jan Ingram, without her knowledge.

Jan was standing by the door greeting her board members as they arrived. She said, "Hello, Dr. Martin. Welcome to the PTA board meeting. It is an honor to have you here today." Katy went over to Jan and whispered, "Thank you for the beautiful surprise in the principal's office. You made a wonderful memory today."

Jan said, "Every sweet word, written by the students, is true."

Jan always made Katy feel that she was special. She frequently told Katy how thankful the parents were to have her as their principal.

Katy said, "Thank you, Jan."

After Katy and Dr. Martin sat down, they continued watching the manner in which Jan interacted with her board members. As Cathy came to the door, they saw Jan hug her. Then they heard Jan ask, "How is Barry? Is he recovering well from his surgery?" Cathy responded with details of his recovery and then thanked Jan for bringing dinner to their house. She said that the chicken casserole was delicious, and it was filled with love.

Next, Barbara came in, and Jan took her hand and said, "Thank you, Barbara, for chairing the open house committee last month. You did an excellent job with this important event." Jan handed her a small gift. It was wrapped in a beautiful floral paper with a pretty bow on top. Jan said, "This is just a little thank you for your leadership and hard work."

Soon the seats were filled, and the attendees were enjoying their chili lunch and visiting with one another. At 12:15 p.m., President Ingram said, "Thank you for being here today. You have numerous tasks on your 'to do' list. Even so, you continue to make the students of Independence High School a high priority in your life. On behalf of these young people, thank you. You are making a positive difference in the lives of our young people.

"Please continue eating and do come back for more chili and dessert. At this time, the meeting will begin. Barbara, thank you for your leadership and hard work with the open house last month. More than one hundred people attended this event, thanks to the stellar planning that took place. Raise your hand if you served on Barbara's committee." Several board members raised their hands. Jan said, "Let's give the committee members a shout-out." In unison, the board members chanted, "I-H-S Team!"

Then, Jan welcomed Dr. Martin, and told him the PTA board wanted to make him an honorary member of the Independence High School PTA. She gave Dr. Martin a PTA pin to make his membership official. He thanked Jan and the board members for the warm welcome and their support of IHS. Then he put the beautiful pin on his lapel, and said, "Thank you for your leadership, and thank you for the delicious lunch." Dr. Martin told the ladies to contact him if he could ever help them in their efforts, and he gave them his email address and cell number.

The board members clapped, and turned their attention to Jan. The president said, "The Visual Arts Event will be here soon. Thank you, Karen, for graciously agreeing to chair this committee. At this time, Karen will provide an update about the event." Karen quickly went through the litany of details to inform her board. When she finished, Jan said, "Thank you, Karen."

A board member raised her hand. Jan called her name, "Yes, Debbie?" Debbie explained an idea she had for an event that could piggyback off of the Visual Arts Event. It was a musical event during lunch one day. Jan said, "Debbie that sounds interesting. Would you like to meet for coffee one day next week to further develop your idea?" Debbie said that sounded like a good idea. Jan said after they met, they would bring more details back to the board for consideration at the next meeting.

Debbie added that if any of the ladies wanted to join Jan and her to please let her know and she would share the place and time for the meeting. Several of the ladies raised their hands or said that they wanted to attend. Debbie wrote their names on her agenda and said, "Thanks, Jan."

Jan smiled and said, "And now, Susan, would you like to review the plans for Teacher Appreciation Week?"

Susan said, "Sure, Jan. Each day next week, the PTA board will create an awareness of how much the parents and students appreciate Independence High School's outstanding teachers. 'Go big or go home'—right, Dr. Carter?

On Monday, a red rose with a blue ribbon will be placed on each teacher's desk with a note that reads: 'The IHS PTA loves you, Beautiful Teacher.'

"On Tuesday, a coffee bar will be set up in the workroom from 7:15 a.m. to 10:00 a.m. Teachers will be invited by putting a Patriot coffee mug in each of their mailboxes with a coupon inside it. The coupon reads: 'Coupon for coffee in the workroom from 7:15 a.m. – 10:00 a.m.'

"On Wednesday, there will be a table in the lunchroom with cupcakes for teacher appreciation. A banner is ready to hang above the table that says, 'A SWEET for our SWEET teachers!' On Thursday, a bottle of water will be placed in each mailbox with a tag that reads, 'Teacher, you refresh others with knowledge and kindness.' And, on Friday, lunch will be provided for the faculty and staff. The menu includes baked ham, sweet potato casserole, green beans, congealed salad, rolls, and turtle cheesecake."

Jan said, "Susan, that is a full week of appreciation, for sure! How wonderful! Does anyone want to make other suggestions for the committee?" Board members made positive comments about the plans and agreed the plans surpassed any teacher appreciation event held at the school.

Jan added, "It will be the best Teacher Appreciation Week ever held at Independence High School. What do you think about adding a line to the cupcake messages that includes support staff? It could say, for example, 'A SWEET for our SWEET teachers, and those who support teachers.'"

Susan said, "Jan, that is an excellent idea, to include the support staff in our appreciation efforts. Does everyone agree?"

The board unanimously agreed by raising their hands and nodding their heads. Jan said, "Wonderful! Let's show our appreciation to Susan and her committee. Ready?" Everyone enthusiastically cheered, "I-H-S Team!"

Jan conducted the business that remained on the agenda and then said, "Before this meeting is adjourned, a quick update is provided about Lynn, a friend and fellow board member. She wanted to be here today, but her chemo treatments are taxing and she is having a difficult time. Please remember Lynn in your thoughts and prayers. There is a 'Get Well' card for Lynn on the table if you would like to sign this card before you leave.

"Are there any other announcements or questions?" No one spoke, and Jan said, "Thank you for coming. Our next meeting with be on the third Wednesday of next month from noon until 1:00 p.m."

Several of the ladies helped clean up after the lunch. They cleaned the conference table and put away all the food. One board member took the remaining ice and drinks to the workroom, while another retrieved a cart from the office. She loaded the cart with the crock-pots and all of Jan's belongings.

Katy and Dr. Martin appeared to remain because they were talking, but actually, they were watching Jan Ingram. They heard a board member ask Jan if anyone was taking food to Lynn, the board member that was fighting cancer. They heard Jan say that she was planning to take food tomorrow. Jan asked the lady if she wanted to go with her. The board member said she couldn't go, but wanted to give money to help with the drinks and bread. Jan said, "How sweet of you. Thank you so much."

At this time, the board members were gone. Dr. Martin told Jan that he enjoyed attending the board meeting, and he thanked her again for the wonderful lunch. Katy also thanked Jan for lunch and told her she would talk to her soon. They offered to help Jan with the cart. She declined and said that was all she had to do. They left the conference room, but remained in sight of the hallway while they were looking at club postings about future events on the hall bulletin board. They saw Jan taking the trash out the back door to the dumpster.

Katy looked at Dr. Martin and said, "Jan doesn't want to add extra work for the custodian tonight. That's why she is taking out the trash." They just looked at each other and shook their heads in amazement. Katy said, "Thank you for coming today, Dr. Martin." He said he enjoyed observing Jan Ingram, a true servant leader, conduct her board meeting. Katy asked, "Do you have time to talk about our observations now?" Dr. Martin said he did. They walked back to the principal's office to meet.

Katy picked up a pen and notepad and sat down at the small conference table. Katy was ready to capture their thoughts about the wise quality of humility. It was a surreal moment for Katy. Her mentor—a successful, enduring leader—sat across from her. Katy, a successful leader and aspiring superintendent, was immersed in the moment. In her heart, she realized the rich rewards of teaching. Nothing could compare with the joy she felt while working with and for her students. Katy could see her students' beautiful letters in her peripheral vision.

Dr. Martin asked, "What is the first example of humble leadership that Jan Ingram displayed?"

Katy said, "She sought input about the PTA board meeting agenda a week before the meeting." Jan cared about Katy's opinion, and made others feel valued.

Dr. Martin added, "She made each board member feel important as well. She was totally engaged with board members—one at a time—as she greeted them when they arrived." Katy wrote as she listened to her superintendent. Dr. Martin said, "President Ingram knew her team members. Ms. Ingram asked one lady how her husband was doing after his surgery. What else did you notice?"

Katy said, "After listening to reports from her committee chairs, she gently added comments, such as including the support staff in the teacher appreciation events."

Dr. Martin said, "That was my favorite part of the meeting. She had a heart for the support staff. She thought of how they might feel when the teachers received a cupcake and they did not."

Katy asked, "Did you notice she had the time of the meeting, *Noon – 1:00 p.m.*, printed on the agenda? You don't see that often. Jan Ingram respected time. She honored the time her board members contributed to the meeting by keeping the meeting going. The meeting never dragged.

"When one board member named Debbie expressed a new idea, Jan invited her to develop the idea in greater detail with her and share it at the next meeting. She did not let her take the meeting hostage with a new idea. And, I noticed that Jan listened more than she spoke."

Dr. Martin agreed. He said, "Ms. Ingram was so gentle and encouraging with that board member. She respectfully listened to her and valued her idea. Jan Ingram is an encourager who has created a safe environment for creativity and collaboration. She makes people feel special." Dr. Martin felt special when he saw the beautiful lunch Jan prepared.

Dr. Martin said, "And, she thinks of others before herself. I will never forget that image of seeing Jan Ingram walking down the hall with the garbage bag."

Katy had tears in her eyes when she said, "She is a humble, wise leader."

He said, "I can see why you identified Jan Ingram as your example of a humble leader." Katy took notes during the PTA board meeting. She asked if he would like for her to read her list of examples of humble leadership that she observed that day. Dr. Martin said, "Yes, please go ahead."

Katy read her list:

Examples of Humility Displayed by the Wise Leader Named Jan Ingram:

1. She values input from others (ideas, time, and effort).
2. She knows her team.
3. She recognizes excellence.
4. She makes others feel special (giving a little gift for committee chair, preparing lunch, student letters for the principal).
5. She encourages others (acknowledges contributions, uplifts team members during challenging times).
6. She listens more than she speaks.
7. She thinks of others before herself (cleaning up after meeting and taking the trash out).
8. She respects others and their contributions (she honors time).

"That is a wonderful summary of Jan Ingram's leadership style. And she is obtaining incredible results. It is evident that board members are excited about being on the PTA board. There was energy in that conference room today, Dr. Carter," Dr. Martin said.

Katy said, "Thank you."

Dr. Martin indicated that he needed to go to his next meeting. He told Katy that at their next meeting they would examine the fifth quality of wise leaders: *self-control*. Katy's mentor gave her an assignment to identify any other proverbs related to humility and email them to him. And Dr. Martin wanted Katy to look for Solomon's wise admonitions for self-control. He said, "Ms. Robertson will contact you to schedule a time to meet again."

Katy said, "That sounds great. Thanks for coming today, Dr. Martin."

THE NEXT MORNING
DURING KATY'S QUIET TIME

The next morning, during Katy's quiet time, Katy reviewed her list of proverbs and identified several that related to the quality of *humility*. She opened her laptop and prepared an email for Dr. Martin:

Dr. Martin,
   After further review, the following proverbs relate to humility:
   Quality #4: Humility

- *When pride comes, then comes disgrace, but with humility comes wisdom.* —Proverbs 11:2
- *A man's pride will bring him low, but a humble spirit will obtain honor.* —Proverbs 29:23, NASB
- *Do not be wise in your own eyes.* —Proverbs 3:7
- *Do you see a man wise in his own eyes? There is more hope for a fool than him.* —Proverbs 26:12
- *Let someone else praise you, and not your own mouth; an outsider, and not your own lips.* —Proverbs 27:2
- *The crucible for silver and the furnace for gold, but people are tested by their praise.* —Proverbs 27:21
- *Do not exalt yourself in the king's presence, and do not claim a place among great men; it is better for him to say to you, "Come up here," than for him to humiliate you before a nobleman.* —Proverbs 25:6–7

Again, thank you for being my mentor.
   Respectfully submitted,
   Katy

Before Katy completed her quiet time (which was increasing each day), she created questions for reflection in her journal:

a. Identify a leader that possesses humility.

b. What qualities does this humble leader consistently exhibit?

c. How do I demonstrate that I value others? Do I seek their input?

d. Am I totally engaged with others as they speak to me? Do I listen more than I speak?

e. List three ways I can be a more humble leader.

f. Do I consider others to be more important than me?

Chapter Five

Quality #5: Wise Leaders Are Self-Controlled

A wise man keeps himself under control. —Proverbs 29:11

It was quiet in the Carters' simple, orderly house on Sunday afternoon. Daniel was playing golf, and Katy easily captured a couple of hours to identify proverbs related to self-control. She began her study time, as usual, with a cup of tea. While the teakettle heated the water, Katy reached for a cup and saucer, nestled among their family of wedding china and crystal goblets in her vintage china cabinet. She selected a favorite cup and saucer—one that she found in an antique store years ago. On the front of the white cup, a bluebird perched on a tree limb.

As she gazed upon the beautiful bird, the teakettle whistled. Katy rescued it from the gas flame and poured boiling water over the green tea bag while she admired the blue interior of the cup—the same color of blue as the bird. After adding lemon and honey, and a sprig of mint from her herb garden, Katy went to her farm table to study, with her back to the southern exposed window. The sun warmed her, and brightly illuminated her journal and attitude. The delightful aroma of the tea and the comforting, calm tea ritual helped her to focus on the task before her.

Katy opened her treasured black journal and looked at her growing list of proverbs. With a freshly sharpened #2 pencil, she placed an asterisk beside the verses related to self-control. Then she sorted them into two groups by placing a one or two in front of the asterisk. The two groups easily identified themselves:

1. *Control of Self*

2. *Control of Self with Others*

She created a master list of the selected proverbs in her journal by group beneath the heading of Quality #5. She provided the main theme of the proverb, the proverb itself, and its chapter and verse:

Quality #5: Wise Leaders Are Self-Controlled

There are two groups of proverbs related to self-control. They include control of self and control of self with others:

1. *Control of Self*

  • *Food (Gluttony)*
    Do not join those who drink too much wine, or gorge themselves on meat, for drunkards and gluttons become poor. —Proverbs 23:20–21
  • *Alcohol*
    It is not for kings to drink wine, not for rulers to crave beer, lest they drink and forget what has been decreed, and deprive all the oppressed of their rights. —Proverbs 31:4–5
  • *Work Ethic*
    Lazy hands make for poverty, but diligent hands bring wealth. —Proverbs 10:4
    A little sleep, a little slumber, a little folding of the hands to rest—and poverty will come on you like a thief. —Proverbs 24:33–34
  • *Sexual Behavior*
    A man who commits adultery lacks judgment. —Proverbs 6:32
  • *Stability*
    If you fall to pieces in a crisis, there wasn't much to you in the first place. —Proverbs 24:10, MSG

2. *Control of Self with Others*

  • *Anger*
    A fool gives full vent to his anger, but a wise man keeps himself under control. —Proverbs 29:11
  • *Answering a Foolish Person*
    Do not answer a fool according to his folly, or you will be like him yourself. —Proverbs 26:4
  • *Patience*
    A person's wisdom yields patience. —Proverbs 19:11
    Better a patient man than a warrior, a man who controls his temper than one who takes a city. —Proverbs 16:32

- *Not Easily Offended*
  It is to one's glory to overlook an offense. —Proverbs 19:11
- *Choosing Friends*
  Do not make friends with a hot-tempered man, do not associate with one easily angered, or you may learn his ways and get yourself ensnared. —Proverbs 22:24–25

Katy quickly thought of a number of wise people who exemplified the self-control Solomon spoke of in the selected proverbs, and she thought of foolish people who did not. First, Katy thought about the students she worked with through the years. She thought of previous class presidents such as Lance, Mack, Sara, Jason, Tyler, and Colby.

These leaders did not choose to be involved in risky teenage behaviors such as drinking alcohol, experimenting with drugs, or engaging in sexual behavior. They were steady individuals who focused on their academic work. As a matter of fact, most were in the top 10 percent academically. Furthermore, these wise student leaders were socially literate individuals who rarely got into altercations with their peers. They carefully picked their friends. They were slow to anger, and not easily offended. They were positive young people who chose to believe the best about others.

When thinking about self-controlled adults, Katy thought of an outstanding teacher named Ms. Robinson. A smile came across her face as she recalled an incident she observed during a special education meeting, between Ms. Robinson and a colleague who was known for being hot-tempered. When he raised his voice as he spoke to Ms. Robinson and pointed his finger in this master teacher's face, she didn't flinch, but simply said in a normal tone of voice, "Remove your finger from in front of my face immediately."

The hot-tempered teacher did immediately remove his finger from in front of her face, and sat down. Ms. Robinson remained calm and defused the situation. She exemplified two proverbs—she was slow to anger and she did not act foolish simply because he was acting foolish.

With regard to foolish behavior, it made Katy sad to think about those students who chose to be friends with the wrong crowd. How many times did parents and teachers try to reach those struggling students, to no avail? It was disheartening to watch. Katy never wanted to give up on a student. Yes, she had several examples of students—one in particular, Jonah, had ended up in jail—who "made friends with a hot-tempered man." And she watched helplessly as he "learned his ways" and became "ensnared."

Jonah was one of the most handsome, strong young men in Dr. Carter's school. He had a tough life without a father. His mother's relentless efforts to steer him in the right direction failed, and he became entrenched in a gang. He enjoyed talking about "his boys" in the gang. He had a record of losing his temper with students, teachers, counselors, and administrators. He was volatile.

Teachers knew Jonah could explode and disrupt the orderly school day at any given moment. One day, this student lost his temper, and when a school resource officer corrected him, Jonah assaulted the officer. This poor decision landed Jonah in juvenile detention. It broke Katy's heart to watch her students struggle and fail.

Thinking about Jonah and wondering what became of him made Katy sad. Even so, it was interesting recalling these incidents and placing them in context with Solomon's proverbs. Truth was revealing itself to Katy through her reflection of experiences that aligned with Solomon's wise proverbs.

The aspiring superintendent closed her journal and turned her attention to the week ahead. Mentally, she thought about high-priority items for the upcoming week, and made a list of them to guide her through Monday. Katy took her cup and saucer to the kitchen, and after placing them in the dishwasher, she decided to take a long walk before starting dinner. It was a beautiful day. She put on her walking shoes, straw hat, and sunglasses, and headed outside, still thinking about Solomon and how he made wise decisions. She took a deep breath and looked up at the beautiful sky.

Solomon—he had it all. Later in life, he wrote in Ecclesiastes 1:18 "For with much wisdom comes much sorrow." She experienced this sorrow when she recognized her own foolish mistakes or watched others make foolish mistakes. There was comfort in having the knowledge to identify foolish behavior, but sorrow emerged when she observed it. One truth was certain for her. She wanted more discipline and wisdom in her life—in all areas. She was a seeker of knowledge, and she was learning from the wisest king that ever lived.

Just thinking about the positive ways her new knowledge was improving her life made Katy smile. She was becoming a better school leader by becoming aware of Solomon's proverbs and incorporating them into her professional and personal life.

MEETING WITH DR. MARTIN
TO DISCUSS SELF-CONTROL

Later in the week, Katy received an email from Dr. Martin's secretary rescheduling their meeting. Instead of meeting in his office as originally scheduled, he would be traveling from a state superintendents' meeting, so he wanted to have a teleconference. Beth wanted to know if this would work, and, if so, what number should the superintendent use to reach her?

Katy replied to her email promptly and gave her the office phone number to use. She had a dedicated phone line in her office—she humorously called it the "bat line"—like Batman had in the movies she watched. Katy wanted to make sure that Dr. Martin could reach her while traveling in the car so this was the phone number she gave to Beth.

When Dr. Martin called Katy was in her office, sitting at her desk reading emails. She had her journal with her and it was opened to the section titled "Quality #5: Wise Leaders Are Self-Controlled."

Dr. Martin said, "Afternoon, Dr. Carter. Is this a good connection? You are on speaker." Katy said, "Yes, Dr. Martin. It is just fine. Thank you for calling."

He replied, "Billy Russell, HR Director, is in the car." They were on their way back from a state superintendents' meeting. They had attended the special meeting to discuss and define priorities for the upcoming legislative session.

After exchanging greetings, Dr. Martin explained that he briefed Billy earlier about Solomon's wise proverbs, and in particular, today's topic of self-control. Dr. Martin asked, "Have you had time to review the proverbs and select those that relate to self-control?"

Katy said, "Yes, and there are numerous proverbs related to this topic."

Katy told the gentlemen how she organized the proverbs by sorting them into two groups: *Control of Self* and *Control of Self with Others*. Dr. Martin said, "Interesting. What topics fall under each of your two groups, Katy?"

Katy answered, "The qualities for *Control of Self* are: food, alcohol, work ethic, sexual behavior, and stability. The qualities for *Control of Self with Others* include: anger, answering a foolish person, patience, not easily offended, and choosing friends. Sexual behavior could actually be included in both lists."

Dr. Martin asked, "Do you have the proverbs before you? Please read them." Katy began reading them one by one. When Katy finished reading the proverbs, Billy shared that he had never read these proverbs before. He found them to be very interesting and filled with truth. He said that several HR cases directly related to these proverbs. Dr. Martin agreed and shared that he could recall cases that directly related to each proverb as well. He asked Katy, "Can you think of examples, Katy?"

Katy said, "Yes, sir."

She gave a quick summary of her examples: the teacher that remained calm when a colleague pointed his finger in her face and raised his voice, the student council president who didn't party and waited until he got married to have a sexual relationship, and Jonah, her student that went to jail because he insisted on being with foolish friends and acting like them.

Katy named Dr. Martin as an example of a leader who remained calm and in control at all times—even in a crisis. She thought about the manner in which Dr. Martin dismissed school during the tornado last year. He remained calm and kept the stakeholders informed. Dr. Martin said, "Thank you." In his efforts to be self-controlled, Dr. Martin said he was intentional in his efforts to be in control of his emotions and actions each day. Furthermore, he tried to avoid any situation that could be misunderstood or set an atmosphere for an inappropriate relationship.

Katy's mentor shared that he and Billy agreed on these standards of operational behavior:

1. They would not ride to conferences in a car alone with a woman other than their wife or family member.
2. They would both have a window in their office door.
3. They would not schedule meetings alone with an individual after hours, unless their secretary was also working late.

Katy said, "That is wise. As you know, similar procedures are in place for our faculty and staff for their relationships with students. There is wisdom in implementing standards or rules for adults as well."

Dr. Martin said, "It is a good practice to simply not be at the office after hours. Leaders should try to manage their time well during each day so that they can go home at 5:00 p.m." Billy said, "That is a good practice, and you are to be commended for your example in this area, Dr. Martin. Other super-intendents often work late and expect the staff to do the same." Dr. Martin said, "Thanks, Billy."

Dr. Martin said, "Good job, Katy, identifying proverbs related to self-control. Now, it is time for you to search for true stories of educational leaders who exhibited poor self-control. Capture examples of what happens when leaders make poor decisions or act foolishly. Email a few of the head-lines/stories you find during your search."

Billy expressed interest in seeing the examples as well. Katy told them she would send the examples to both of them soon, and she thanked them for their time. She enjoyed the conversation. Billy agreed and said, "This has been an intellectually stimulating conversation, for sure." He planned on reading more about Solomon and his proverbs after participating in this conversation.

Dr. Martin told Billy and Katy that he planned to discuss the next qual-ity—wise leaders seek counsel—at the next monthly principals' meeting. Katy was already looking forward to learning about the wisdom in seeking counsel.

There were no school activities that afternoon and evening, so Katy and Daniel enjoyed being at home and preparing supper. While Daniel grilled hamburgers, Katy made homemade vanilla ice cream. They enjoyed simple meals. What could be better than a grilled hamburger, a bag of potato chips, and homemade ice cream for dessert? After supper, Katy headed for her beloved back porch with her laptop and sat in her swing. She leaned against a big pillow and relaxed.

Katy took a deep breath and turned sideways so she could put her legs up on the swing, as she began browsing the Internet for topics such as "superintendents + fired + sexual" or "superintendents + temper" or "superintendents + alcohol." She was amazed at the number of news stories that popped up when researched. Katy read the stories and started a list of headlines by copying and pasting the headlines into a Word document. The next morning she sent an email to Dr. Martin and Billy Russell. It said,

Good Morning, Gentlemen:

It was a pleasure to discuss proverbs with you that are related to wise leaders having self-control. Last night, as requested, this aspiring superintendent searched for headlines related to superintendents and educators who demonstrated a lack of self-control. It was amazing to see the number of stories that emerged. See below for a list:

"(District name) teacher who drank alcohol on field trip fired . . ."

"(District name) county schools superintendent arrested for DUI . . ."

"Personal drinking photos could get teachers fired . . ."

"DWI arrest only one reason (name of school district) district seeks firing of superintendent . . ."

"Superintendent fired amid sexual harassment claims . . ."

"(District name) superintendent fired for sexual misconduct . . ."

"(District name) teacher accused of sexually assaulting a student . . ."

"Ousted (district name) deputy superintendent faces sex charges . . ."

"(District name) school superintendent apologizes for losing his temper, using inappropriate language . . ."

"Allegation of superintendent's affair spurs petition . . ."

The proverbs we reviewed and discussed are wise reminders for appropriate behavior, indeed. These examples of poor judgment can happen in any school district. It seems that the reporters like to identify the school district in the headline. This review is eye opening and makes me want to be more vigilant in my professional and personal practices. Thanks again for another inspiring lesson on wise leadership, according to Solomon.

With warmest regards,

Katy

Within twenty-four hours, Katy received a reply from her mentor:

To: Katy

CC: Billy

Hello Katy,

Excellent job:

1. capturing proverbs related to self-control,

2. connecting these proverbs to real people who came into your life who serve as examples of these wise proverbs, and

3. finding true headlines of sad stories that happened in real life in which leaders did not exhibit self-control.

—R.M.

Billy replied to both Katy and Dr. Martin:

Dr. Carter,
  Wow! Your list of headlines serves as a reminder that I must be vigilant in my determination to possess control of myself and control of myself with others. Again, I enjoyed our talk about the proverbs. Thank you, Dr. Martin, for including me in your study. I am also now reading proverbs each day.
  —Billy

During Katy's quiet time of reflection, she captured the following questions in her journal:
  Quality #5: Wise Leaders Are Self-Controlled

  a. What are the two groups of proverbs related to self-control?
  b. List the five themes from the two groups related to self-control.
  c. From headlines in the news, find and list three examples of educational leaders who did not exhibit self-control.
  d. List three to five proverbs that help you remember the importance of self-control, not only with self, but with others.

Chapter Six

Quality #6: Wise Leaders Seek Counsel

Plans fail for lack of counsel, but with many advisors they succeed.
—Proverbs 15:22

Each month, Dr. Martin held a meeting with the principals and district administrators. The yearly schedule for these meetings was distributed in June so that the participants could keep the first Tuesday of the month open for this important half-day meeting. Principals appreciated having meeting dates well in advance so they could schedule school events appropriately.

The principals' meetings were usually held in the boardroom. But Dr. Martin sometimes held the monthly meeting in a unique place such as the Holt home—one of the largest estates in the county. The Holts enjoyed having guests in their home and invited Dr. Martin to host meetings in their dining room when he wanted to do so.

Once, he held the meeting on the football field. In the summer months, Dr. Martin scheduled their meetings at parks or retreat centers so they could share information in a relaxed environment. They grilled hotdogs and enjoyed the beautiful scenery. He encouraged the leaders to wear school t-shirts and tennis shoes for walking during their breaks.

Their school district was small, only five schools, so when they met in a traditional setting it was easy for all of the principals and administrators to meet around a large conference table in the back of the boardroom. This is where the meeting was to be held today. Beth Robertson, the executive secretary to the superintendent, thoughtfully ensured that coffee, water, and snacks were available during these meetings. The administrators worked well together and, for the most part, were a strong, healthy team. They enjoyed the collegiality when they were together.

Katy arrived at 8:20 a.m. just as planned. She liked to leave a few minutes early for her appointments so that she had a margin in her daily schedule. She enjoyed arriving a few minutes early so that she could go to the restroom or get a cup of coffee before the meeting began. Because she usually started her day at 5:00 a.m., by the time she arrived for the 8:30 a.m. meeting she was ready for a reprieve from the morning's demands.

It was nice to sit and enjoy a hot cup of coffee. And now, she took a deep breath and reached for her phone in order to silence it. The school secretary, Ms. Perkins, knew where Katy was, and if an emergency occurred she would contact Beth Robertson in the superintendent's office if she needed to reach Dr. Carter. This principal liked to totally focus on the meeting before her and not be constantly checking her phone for texts and emails.

At 8:20 a.m. Superintendent Ronnie Martin, an inspiring leader and role model, walked into the boardroom. Katy was observant. She noticed that Dr. Martin dressed professionally. He wore a coat and tie and dress shoes. She looked around the room with refreshed vision and saw other leaders—her friends and colleagues—who were dressed professionally and appropriately as well. It was important for school leaders to set the tone through their personal appearance, words, and actions.

The agenda for the meeting was placed on the table in front of each leader's seat. Dr. Carter was not surprised to see the professionally prepared agenda, because Dr. Martin consistently displayed strength in the organizational arena. Katy glanced at the agenda. It was identical to the one Ms. Robertson emailed a few days in advance so that the participants could be prepared for the meeting. This preview of the agenda saved time and effort.

Today's agenda revealed that Dr. Martin would share information regarding strategic planning. Each principal was directed to bring his or her school's improvement plan based on the district's last strategic planning and accreditation process. A copy of the Washington County Schools Strategic Plan and the District Accreditation Report was tucked neatly behind the agenda.

Dr. Martin smiled and shook hands with each administrator, Katy noted. The superintendent began the meeting promptly at 8:30 a.m. by welcoming everyone. Then he sat down at the head of the table and began to speak. The leaders listened carefully and took notes. Their body language revealed total engagement: pleasant facial expressions, eyes on their respected leader, and pens in hands or tablets in place for note-taking. They had all silenced their cell phones.

Dr. Martin provided an overview of the agenda. He said, "Strategic planning is right around the corner. It is listed before you now on the agenda simply to create an awareness of its importance and its impending arrival next year. Input will be solicited from stakeholders in the spring through surveys and meetings. This will offer opportunities for discussion about the state of our school district. Then, we will begin evaluating the data during the summer.

"It is the perfect time to review the current strategic plan, along with the accreditation report, in order to create questions to include in the proposed survey. In your packet, please find draft survey questions. Please review these questions. As always, your input is solicited and respected. You may want to add, edit, or delete a question."

Dr. Martin extracted the proposed survey as he spoke. Katy reviewed the draft survey along with her colleagues as they listened to their superintendent. Dr. Martin seemed to be consistently one step ahead—proactive—just like the wise leaders Katy studied with him, she noted.

The superintendent continued talking after sharing the draft document. "It is important and wise to seek input. According to the Bible, Solomon was the wisest king that ever lived. He shared his wisdom through the proverbs he penned. Solomon said, 'Plans fail for lack of counsel, but with many advisors, plans succeed.' He also said, 'Where there is no vision, the people perish.'

"It is of utmost importance to provide a vision for this school district. This team is charged with the responsibility of creating the plan for continual school improvement in Washington County Schools. Stakeholders must be given the opportunity to provide input. After listening carefully to all stakeholders, the school district will move forward with its efforts to continually improve. Who are the stakeholders?" An elementary principal, Dr. Bo Scott, raised his hand to answer the question.

Dr. Martin called his name. Bo said, "Stakeholders include community members, parents, teachers, support staff, and students."

Dr. Martin replied, "Absolutely. And each of these groups will be included in our planning and review efforts. Why should the strategic plan be revisited?"

John Perry, a middle school principal, said, "Leaders seek continual school improvement for the benefit of students. The school district should offer the best education possible for them." Dr. Martin smiled and said, "That's right. All work is for the students' benefit. Leaders are charged with the daunting task of preparing them for the future. Excellence is pursued in order to provide the best educational opportunities possible for our deserving students."

The meeting continued with a presentation from Billy Russell, the HR director. Mr. Russell reviewed standard accounting procedures and board policy related to collecting and depositing funds through athletic events and fund-raisers. Katy was aware of the information he shared, but she found it helpful to review it. She wanted to keep a watchful eye on all areas entrusted to her care.

When the meeting ended, Dr. Martin walked over to Katy and said, "Are you interested in meeting a superintendent who exemplifies the proverbs: 'As iron sharpens iron, so one man sharpens another,' and 'Wisdom is found in those who take advice'?"

Katy said, "Yes, that sounds like a wonderful opportunity."

He explained that he wanted Katy to meet Dr. Sandra Spivey so she could hear her story of seeking counsel. Dr. Martin saw Dr. Spivey at the state superintendents' meeting a couple of weeks ago, and he told her about Katy's quest to become a superintendent. Dr. Martin told Katy, "She seemed genuinely pleased to have the opportunity to meet you. Ms. Robertson will send you Dr. Spivey's contact information. You will enjoy and benefit from hearing Sandra's interesting story.

"Additionally, the two of you have common interests. And it's never a bad idea to make new friendships and connections."

Katy said, "Thank you, Dr. Martin." That afternoon, as promised, Katy received the contact information for Dr. Spivey from Dr. Martin's executive secretary. After creating a new contact, Katy immediately emailed Dr. Spivey:

Dr. Spivey,
Thank you in advance for agreeing to meet with me at Dr. Martin's suggestion. May we meet face-to-face at your office? I look forward to hearing from you, and I can't wait to hear your story of seeking counsel.
With warmest regards,
Katy Carter

The next morning, Katy found a reply to her email from Dr. Spivey. She had written,

Hi, Katy. I would be delighted to meet with you. I've heard nice comments about you and I look forward to getting to know you and sharing my journey to the superintendent's office. Are you available to meet in my office on Monday afternoon at 2:00 p.m.?
Best,
Sandra

Katy was able to meet at the time suggested. She quickly responded to Dr. Spivey's kind invitation to confirm the date and time, and she added the meeting information to her digital calendar. Now, she turned her attention to a classroom observation for the chemistry teacher, Ms. May. There would be time to prepare for her meeting with Dr. Spivey later in the week.

KATY MEETS DR. SPIVEY

Monday was actually a good day for Katy to meet with Dr. Spivey. It was a quiet week at Independence High School. Dr. Spivey's school district was sixty-three miles east of Washington County. Katy allowed two hours for the drive, so she would have that margin in her schedule. She felt more relaxed when she buffered her schedule with extra time. Katy felt that being rushed was stressful and unproductive. She was pleased with her new practice of adding twenty to thirty minutes between meetings so that she could transition in a relaxed, professional manner.

The drive was especially enjoyable because of the spectacular landscape. Katy's car was nestled among the majestic Appalachian Mountains and the highway upon which she traveled paralleled the serene Tennessee River. The peaceful river reflected the sunshine upon its smooth surface, while stoic fishermen sat in their boats, patiently waiting for fish to take a bite.

Intentionally, Katy drove in silence. She took several deep breaths and relaxed as she thought about her personal and professional life. Kathleen Estelle Olive Carter was happy. She was healthy. She was grateful for the blessings in her life. She started calling the blessings by name.

She was thankful for her faith, husband, family, meaningful work with children, education, friends, health, home, material blessings—like the bed she slept in last night and her car and clothes—vacations, special people like her mentor, this beautiful day, animals, holidays, music, and beauty in nature. She smiled as she meditated on the gifts she received in life. She thought about what the future might hold for her if she became a superintendent. How would life be different from now? She was looking forward to the journey, if selected for this key leadership post.

Before she realized it, an hour evaporated, and Katy was in close vicinity of Dr. Spivey's office. She made a quick stop to freshen up for her meeting. When she arrived at her destination, she found the board of education facility to be well maintained. She observed a clean campus and manicured landscaping. An attractive rug, with the district crest proudly displayed in its center, allowed her to wipe her shoes off before stepping inside onto the polished tile floor.

Inside, Katy found students' colorful artwork displayed on the wall adjacent to the superintendent's office. Just as Katy was examining the creative art, Dr. Spivey walked out to meet Katy, right on time. She said, "Dr. Carter, it is an honor to meet you. Your reputation and stellar career in Washington County precede you. Welcome."

Katy replied, "You are kind, Dr. Spivey. What a pleasure it is to meet you." Dr. Spivey offered Katy water or coffee as they walked into her office. Katy thanked her, but declined. She sat down at the conference table after pausing to allow Dr. Spivey to choose her seat, and placed her black journal on the table in front of her. She noticed an inviting, warm, attractive, and organized office.

Dr. Spivey's large desk was neat, reflecting the careful oversight of its owner. The bookcases behind her desk showcased Sandra Spivey's collection of books. Katy noticed blank space in the bookcases also, as if Dr. Spivey intentionally saved space for future growth. She liked this notion. A ficus tree, flourishing in the corner beside the window, provided relief from the academic nature of the office, and a potted philodendron announced that it was indeed healthy, as it happily spilled out of its ceramic pot and trailed down the window's ledge.

Katy had noticed Dr. Spivey's professional attire as they walked to the superintendent's office. She wore a navy blue skirt with a pale yellow blouse, gray jacket, closed-toe black pumps, and minimal jewelry. Dr. Spivey was a classic professional, Katy thought. There was nothing flashy about her. Dr. Spivey was well groomed. Her short hair was attractive and simple.

Katy asked Dr. Spivey for permission to take notes while they talked, and Dr. Spivey readily agreed. Katy extracted two sheets of paper—one for Dr. Spivey and one for herself—that captured the questions she wanted to ask. Katy read the first question as their eyes gazed upon the prepared document:

"1. How did you determine that you wanted to become a superintendent?"

Dr. Spivey demonstrated superior communication skills. She was articulate and relaxed. She displayed positive body language as she made eye contact with Katy and explained that before ever deciding to apply for a superintendent's position, she talked with her husband, and prayed about it. She knew she would not just apply for every position that became available, but would consider a lot of factors in the decision. Location was important, because she did not want to ask her husband to leave his job again as he had willingly done several times.

Dr. Spivey sought advice from only a small group of wise leaders for whom she had great respect, because they were godly people, proven leaders who were willing to spend time mentoring aspiring leaders, and good listeners who gave useful guidance/advice. Also, she found these selected advisors to be trustworthy and kind.

Katy said, "Your answer reminds me of Solomon's proverb that states, 'Wisdom is found in those who take advice.'"

Dr. Spivey replied, "It does, doesn't it? There is another proverb that states, 'Plans fail for lack of counsel, but with many advisors they succeed.'"

Katy nodded her head in agreement and said, "Yes, that proverb is captured in ink within the pages of my journal. Did Dr. Martin tell you about our review of Solomon's proverbs?"

Dr. Spivey said, "Yes, he did. Dr. Martin actually told me about Solomon's proverbs several years ago." She was transparent in sharing her affection for Solomon's proverbs. Dr. Spivey said that she continued to embrace them through regular review since that time.

Katy said, "Dr. Martin said that you are an example of one who seeks advice. He respects and admires you or he would not have arranged this meeting."

Sandra replied, "Thank you. Ronnie Martin is a wise leader who serves as a role model for many superintendents in our state."

Katy said, "It is an honor to be mentored by him. Question number two: How did you prepare for your interview and site visit once you were selected as a finalist for the superintendent position?"

Before beginning the process of applying for superintendent positions, Dr. Spivey carefully updated her resume, letter of interest, letters of recommendation, and so forth, and created an informational packet to give to each board member. She reread a book that had an impact on her several years ago: *The Servant*, by James C. Hunter. She also revisited her educational philosophy and researched some commonly asked interview questions. She prepared responses to help her think through the various issues that she might be asked to address.

Dr. Spivey explained that she also reviewed all the data that she could obtain on the school district through the system's website and the State Department of Education. Usually, it is easy to find a report card on each district and school. Then, she researched the city and county in which the system was located. From this review, Dr. Spivey gleaned population and demographic data, and specifics on the school district. This research proved helpful to her. The board members did not expect Dr. Spivey to know everything about their school system, but she was able to utilize data such as test scores and graduation rates during her initial interview.

When she learned that she was a finalist for her current position as superintendent, she met with her mentor, Dr. Ronnie Martin, and asked for advice about interviewing. From that conversation, she got the idea to prepare a portfolio. "It provided the inspiration for my collection of artifacts," she said.

The creation of that portfolio helped her reflect and prepare for the interview. Dr. Spivey revealed her belief that it made a difference in the selection process. She would not have thought to create that portfolio without the wise counsel she received. Dr. Spivey asked Katy, "Would you like to see the portfolio?"

Katy enthusiastically replied, "Yes. Thank you."

Dr. Spivey retrieved the portfolio from her organized bookcase and carefully placed it before Katy. She let Katy review it while she said hello to a group of teachers who were meeting next door. Katy glanced at her watch, being ever mindful of the superintendent's time and her own. She began to look at the contents of the beautiful, professional portfolio before her as the superintendent left the room.

The documents were organized into sections in the table of contents. In the first section Dr. Spivey had listed *Letter to School Board Members*, *Resume*, and *Professional Certificates*. In the next section, she included personal information about where she grew up, and her faith and family. The next few sections included information related to each position Dr. Spivey held in her professional career. These sections highlighted the position held, accomplishments from this period of work, newspaper articles, and letters of recommendation.

The last section, titled "What You Can Expect from Me if I Am Selected to Be Your Next Superintendent," contained seventeen important areas of responsibility along with a brief summary of expectations related to these subgroups:

1. Communication
2. Community
3. Leadership
4. Superintendent and School Board Relationships
5. Fiscal Management
6. Human Resources
7. Safety
8. Technology
9. Co-Curricular Activities
10. Fine Arts
11. Athletics
12. Career and Technical Education
13. Special Education, etc.
14. The State's Strategic Plan
15. Accountability
16. Ninety-Day Plan of Action
17. Commitment to the Board of Education

Katy was incredibly impressed with the professional portfolio created by Dr. Sandra Spivey. It was exemplary. After quickly reviewing the first seven sections, she turned to section eight and began to read.

Katy thought to herself, "It is no wonder that Dr. Spivey was selected for this important leadership position. What an impressive display of credentials, organization, and communication." Katy turned to section one in the portfolio and reviewed the letter Dr. Spivey wrote to the board of education members. It read:

Scottsboro City School System Board Members:
I want to thank you for considering me as a candidate for the superintendent's position in the Scottsboro City School System. I am truly honored to be

selected as a finalist. Before applying for the position, I carefully reviewed the system's statement regarding the "characteristics and qualities sought in the new superintendent," and after thoughtful examination, I became convinced that I am qualified for consideration as a viable candidate for the job. I believe that I am contributing in a positive way in my current role as the Regional Support Coordinator (Regions 3 and 5) for the Alabama State Department of Education, and that I have also made a positive impact in other administrative positions in Madison County, Hoover, and Alexander City.

In previous roles, I had the privilege of working collaboratively with all of the employees at the district level, as well as with the faculty and staff members in the schools. In my current role, I now have the opportunity to work with many school systems across the state to provide support and assistance as they work to make improvements and achieve short- and long-term goals. I am very interested in taking on the additional responsibilities of a superintendent and working in that capacity to ensure the achievement of district-wide goals and objectives.

I was born and raised in Scottsboro and, as a graduate of Scottsboro High School who completed all of my years of public education (first through twelfth grade) in the Scottsboro City School System, I have a particular sense of pride in the schools and community. The Scottsboro City School System is a very good school system with much potential for continued growth and excellence. I believe that I have the training, experience, personality, and work ethic that would enable me to make a positive difference as the superintendent of Scottsboro City Schools, and it would be my privilege to be selected to fill this very important role.

I have compiled some information that, in addition to my visit to Scottsboro and interview today, will hopefully provide a clearer picture of who I am personally and professionally. Please let me know if I can provide any other information that you need as you work through this process. I truly appreciate your consideration of my candidacy for this very important employment decision.

Sincerely,

Sandra W. Spivey, EdD

Katy especially liked the heart-warming personal memorabilia that Dr. Spivey included in each section. She also declared the section about Benjamin Russell High School, where Dr. Spivey served as a teacher, assistant principal, and principal, her personal favorite section of the portfolio. Katy admired Dr. Spivey and her many contributions to the lives of children in the field of education. She was gazing at this section when Dr. Spivey returned to the office.

Katy looked at Dr. Spivey and said, "Your beautiful portfolio is amazing. You provided in-depth personal information that allowed board members an opportunity to make a personal connection with you and get to know you."

Dr. Spivey said she enjoyed making it for them, and would always treasure the portfolio as a keepsake of her career. She laughed when she said, "The cover of my portfolio should read, *This is Your Life!*" They both laughed.

Katy thanked Sandra Spivey for sharing her portfolio. She enjoyed reviewing it because she learned a tremendous amount about communication and revealing oneself to the members of the board. Katy asked Dr. Spivey if she had time for one final question. Sandra smiled and said, "Of course." Katy was watchful of Dr. Spivey's body language. She didn't seem hurried. She sat back down at the conference table and looked at Katy.

Katy asked Dr. Spivey if she had any advice for her as she began the process of seeking a superintendent position. Dr. Spivey was vulnerable with Katy when she acknowledged that she applied for four previous superintendent positions before being selected. She was not selected for three of the four, and she removed herself from the process in one system after seeing some things that concerned her. Dr. Spivey said she learned different lessons throughout the process, and she carried that learning forward as she continued in her leadership roles.

Because of her reflective nature, Dr. Spivey knew that if God intended for her to have the job in each case, it would happen, and if not, she would learn from it. When making the decision to apply for each position, she made a list of the pros and cons. She loved the jobs she was doing at the time of each application, so part of the deliberation involved thinking about leaving the job/people she loved.

Often that part is not considered when people consider applying for new jobs. Or sometimes people are trying to "get away from" a situation by pursuing another job; in that case, Sandra said people have to be careful that they don't "jump out of the frying pan and into the fire." Dr. Spivey said that one of the things she learned over time was to not allow praise or criticism to change her outlook.

It is easy to listen to compliments/praise and allow that to cloud judgment, in the same way that it is easy to listen to criticism/negativity and allow that to cloud judgment. Dr. Spivey said, "*It is better to remain steady* while reflecting on experiences and seeking wise counsel. And *it is better not to ask for advice at all unless you ask for advice from a wise person. Otherwise, the advice you get can just 'muddy the waters' and cause more harm than good.*"

Katy thanked Sandra for taking time to meet with her. Their time went by so quickly, and Katy learned valuable lessons from meeting with Dr. Spivey. She didn't know how she could ever repay her. Dr. Spivey said, "Thank you.

Just pay it forward. Help an aspiring administrator as you go along your journey."

Katy promised she would do so. As she picked up her things to leave, Sandra gave her business card with her cell phone number on it to Katy. She wished Katy good luck and told Katy to call her if she could support her in any way. Katy was deeply touched and said, "Thank you so much, Dr. Spivey."

Dr. Spivey smiled and said, "Please call me Sandra."

Katy listened to classical music on the way home as the sun went quietly behind the mountains. The day was coming to its end. And what a day it had been. Meeting Dr. Spivey was a highlight she would never forget. Katy thought about the demands of the superintendency, and how this precious lady carried the load with grace. She generously gave of herself to help another leader who aspired to become a superintendent.

One day, Katy thought, she would be a superintendent and she would stop and take time to notice other people. She would take time to encourage them and befriend them. Katy was filled with gratitude for those who had taken time to help her: Dr. Martin, Mr. Coleman, Dr. Carroll, and now Dr. Spivey.

AFTER THE MEETING WITH DR. SPIVEY

After Thanksgiving, Katy was back to her normal school schedule. It was 3:30 p.m., and she was at her desk planning for the last few weeks of the calendar year, which was also the end of the school semester. As Dr. Carter created a list of important tasks to complete, she paused to reflect on the numerous lessons she learned since Dr. Martin became her mentor. She had her black journal in her school bag. She was about to retrieve her journal, and then she thought about taking a walk.

It was a pretty day, even though it was cool. This principal needed a walk because she had been sitting in meeting after meeting that day. And sitting at a conference table tired her. Dr. Carter was vibrant and full of energy; she enjoyed being physically active.

So Katy grabbed her coat, scarf, and bag, and headed out the door. She always wore smart shoes to work each day. Because she was on her feet a lot, Katy invested in comfortable, good-looking shoes. She could easily walk a mile in her work shoes. She had an hour and a half until she planned to meet Daniel for a spaghetti supper at Lombardo's, before the 7:00 p.m. band concert. She decided to take a walk to the local coffee shop two blocks from Independence High School.

As the Independence High School principal strolled from school to coffee shop, she observed her lovely town and she thought about the night ahead. She was looking forward to the IHS band concert that night.

The community supported the school. The auditorium would be packed as usual, she predicted. The music would be lively. She couldn't wait to see her students on stage performing. She couldn't wait to get lost in their beautiful music. The Independence Ambassadors, students who represented the high school, would be dressed in black as they always were, but tonight they were all planning to wear Santa hats as they greeted guests and distributed the concert programs.

It was quiet in Berkeley Bob's Coffee Shop when Katy arrived. There was an empty café table in the back right corner, and Katy walked over to it and laid her bag and coat on the chair. She walked to the counter and said, "Hi, Julie. May I have an Americano, please?"

Julie replied, "Coming right up."

Katy placed four dollars on the counter and said, "This is good—keep the change." Katy needed a little boost of energy and this shot of brewed espresso with hot water would be just what the doctor ordered.

Katy sat down at her table and took a deep breath. She opened her bag and removed her journal as she began reviewing the lessons she had learned about wise leadership. By the time Katy was immersed in her notes, Bob, the owner of the coffee shop, walked over to Katy's table and carefully sat her black coffee cup in front of her. Printed on the mug was a picture of a snazzy sports car with the caption "Washington's Auto Body and Frame" beneath it. On the backside of the mug, the address, phone number and website for Washington's was listed. Katy loved the variety of Bob's mugs—the donated mugs were from local businesses.

Bob asked, "How's everything at the high school?"

Katy smiled and said, "The students are dreading semester exams, but looking forward to a two-week break during the holidays. Remember those days, Bob?"

Bob nodded his head and said, "Enjoy your coffee, and thanks for all you do for kids, Katy."

Katy said, "Thanks a lot, Bob." Katy took a sip of the hot coffee and relaxed, sinking into this treasured time of rest and reflection.

Reflection

With a black calligraphy pen in hand, Katy wrote beautifully in her journal:

Quality #6: Wise Leaders Seek Counsel.

She thought of all the people with whom she worked. She thought about her behavior and performance throughout her career. She posed the following reflective questions:

1. *Identify one person who seeks counsel. How or why did this person seek advice or counsel?*
2. *Have I ever sought input or advice from others in order to make a plan for improvement?*
3. *If so, how did I seek their advice? Face-to-face meeting? Survey? Email?*
4. *How did Dr. Spivey incorporate the advice she received into her plan for applying for superintendent?*

Katy thought about Dr. Spivey seeking Dr. Martin's counsel when she was selected as a finalist for the superintendent position. She thought about her last principals' meeting when reflecting on question two. She looked forward to seeking input from stakeholders regarding the high school. She thought about Daniel and the question he sometimes asked her. She noticed when she had a busy day or week or a special event, her sweet husband might ask how he could make her day or week better. He was seeking ways to improve their quality of life, Katy thought. She was thankful to have her supportive husband.

She was glad she asked Dr. Martin to be her mentor to provide advice for her career. She wrote the names of Daniel, Dr. Martin, Dr. Spivey, and the word "Stakeholders" in the space below question two. This list included personal and professional requests for advice. She liked face-to-face meetings and stated that fact under question three. Although it wasn't imperative, it was more personal.

And, under the last question for reflection, Katy wrote, "*Dr. Sandra Spivey is a wise leader. She asked for input from a few trusted advisors. Using their counsel, she developed her plan for her upcoming interview, along with the documents she wished to provide. She created a portfolio based on the idea she garnered from a meeting with her mentor.*"

Katy closed her journal. Her black coffee cup was empty; an hour had passed. It was time to walk back to school to meet Daniel for supper. Katy was refreshed from her walk and inspired from her time of reflection. And now, she looked forward to a relaxing Italian dinner with her husband, and the band concert afterwards.

Chapter Seven

Quality #7: Wise Leaders Understand Others

Be sure you know the condition of your flocks . . . —Proverbs 27:23

Before the conclusion of the week, Katy heard from Dr. Martin's secretary, Beth Robertson, via email:

> Subject: Appointment with Dr. Martin
> Dr. Carter,
> Dr. Martin wishes to convey to you that he received your kind note thanking him for his time and effort in arranging for you to meet Dr. Spivey. Dr. Spivey called him to say that she enjoyed meeting you, and that she received and appreciated your thoughtful card as well.
> He would like to meet with you and Billy Russell next Tuesday at 3:30 p.m. at his office to discuss Quality #7: Wise Leaders Understand Others. Please let me know if this is a convenient time for you.
> Thank you,
> Beth Robertson
> Executive Secretary to the Superintendent

Katy reviewed her calendar and quickly confirmed the suggested meeting time in an email reply to Beth. She looked forward to hearing about the seventh and final quality of wise leaders. Katy continued to benefit from her study of Proverbs. Thanks to Dr. Martin, she now possessed an awareness of Solomon's wise admonitions. Katy yearned to put his proverbs into practice each day in her service as principal—and, hopefully, one day as superintendent. Katy Carter truly wanted to be the best she could be as she labored to improve the lives of her students.

Additionally, she wanted to incorporate Solomon's proverbs into her personal life as she strived to make wise decisions and be a blessing to others. Katy wondered how Dr. Martin would connect the quality of understanding to Solomon's proverbs. Prior to the meeting, Katy reviewed the long list of proverbs that she had previously captured in her journal. Then she highlighted the proverbs that she thought pertained to the topic of understanding.

THE MEETING—DR. MARTIN'S OFFICE

When Katy arrived at Dr. Martin's office, Beth greeted her warmly and immediately escorted her into the superintendent's office, where she found Billy Russell seated at the conference table with her mentor. Both gentlemen stood when she entered the room. As they did so, Katy remembered one of George Washington's rules of civility: *Sit not when others stand.* Dr. Martin, a history buff, admired President George Washington and often quoted him. After all, their county was named after this outstanding leader. Katy greeted the two gentlemen as she walked toward the large, round table that was surrounded by six Federal-style mahogany chairs.

Katy noticed the details in the superintendent's professional office: the uncluttered environment, the well-maintained interior, the bright lights illuminating the conference table, and the sparkling windows that were clothed with venetian blinds. The dark navy rug in front of Dr. Martin's desk proudly displayed their school district's crest in its center. On the back wall, Katy noticed the gold, wooden letters mounted with precision. They united to spell the name of their beloved school district: WASHINGTON COUNTY.

The right wall, perpendicular to the wall behind his desk, showcased two patriotic flags that anchored simple bookcases: the American flag properly stood on the left while the state flag properly stood on the right.

George Washington was Dr. Martin's favorite president. As such, he liked to incorporate trivia about the president into his speeches. And, here in the superintendent's office, Katy saw a reflection of that admiration revealed. A Colonial brass table lamp, topped with a black shade, proudly illuminated Dr. Martin's desktop, while two black captain's chairs faced the stately, antique partners' desk. Behind the superintendent's desk, reverently hanging on the wall above the credenza, Katy saw a fine portrait of America's first president, General George Washington. Katy, one who appreciated attention to detail, said, "Dr. Martin, your office is beautiful."

Dr. Martin replied, "Thank you, Dr. Carter. Did you know that my office is painted in the same colors as George and Martha Washington's master bedroom?"

Katy said, "No, sir. That is interesting."

Dr. Martin continued, "Yes, it's true. This historical color combination of off-white walls with Colonial blue paint trim is calming. Do you agree?"

Katy replied in agreement. "Yes, it is a soothing color, indeed."

Dr. Martin, pointing to his desk, said, "Sitting on top of that thin stack of papers is a cast-iron replica of the key to the Bastille." He walked over to the desk and picked up the heavy key, then handed the artifact that dually served as a paperweight to Katy. Dr. Martin said, "It was a gift from a colleague who visited Mount Vernon. The original key is displayed in the foyer of George and Martha Washington's home. The Marquis de Lafayette gave the key to George Washington in 1790, after the destruction of the Bastille prison in Paris."

Katy said, "How interesting." She noticed his laptop was atop a standing desk on the left side of his office. Katy enjoyed seeing functional, inspiring workspaces such as Dr. Martin's office. And she also liked incorporating school spirit into her office. Often, before a meeting began, Katy tried to make a connection with stakeholders by talking about an item in her office such as her photo wall or student artwork to help "break the ice."

UNDERSTANDING

Dr. Martin walked toward the conference table, where a prepared handout waited. Katy redirected her attention to Dr. Martin as he distributed a sheet of paper with the heading, *A List of Proverbs Related to Quality #7: Understanding*, to each of them. They were now seated at the table. Katy looked at the list and saw that the proverbs were divided into four sections:

1. Understanding of Self and Others
2. Displaying Understanding through Words
3. Displaying Understanding through Actions
4. A Word of Caution

Her mentor explained that they were there to continue their conversation on wise leadership, according to Solomon. Through his reading of Solomon's proverbs, and through his observations of others and reflection on his own experiences, he believed that enduring, successful leaders possessed seven qualities. They had studied the first six qualities that these wise leaders seem to possess:

1. Vision
2. Knowledge
3. Ethics
4. Humility

---

5. Self-control
6. Counsel

Today they planned to talk about the last quality that wise leaders seemed to possess:

1. Understanding

Dr. Martin said, "Billy wants to participate in this last session because his interest in Solomon's proverbs is growing. In his role as HR director, he must understand others. He must possess stellar interpersonal relationship skills. And this last quality that wise leaders possess is directly related to maintaining stellar interpersonal relationships or working with others in a positive manner." Billy nodded his head in agreement.

Katy listened intently as her mentor continued: "Look at the handout. The list of proverbs is divided into four sections: 'Understanding Self and Others,' 'Displaying Understanding through Words,' 'Displaying Understanding through Actions,' and 'A Word of Caution.' *Leaders seek to understand others. They display their understanding through their words and actions toward others.*"

1. UNDERSTANDING SELF AND OTHERS

"First, let's talk about understanding self and others. Leaders cannot seek to understand others until they understand themselves. The wise leader is always mindful of *his own* condition. King Solomon said, '*Be sure you know the condition of your flocks.*' The watchful eyes of the wise leader are ever upon his team, while at the same time he is mindful of the condition of individual team members. The wise leader can examine his condition and the condition of others while observing his team through the lenses of special glasses—the PIES glasses. The leader can look through four different lenses:
P – Physical
I – Intellectual
E – Emotional
S – Spiritual
"When the wise leader sees a team member struggling, he asks himself:

- Why is this person struggling? Is he or she sick? (Physical)
- Is this person struggling because of work overload, or is the work too difficult? Or perhaps the person is pursuing graduate work? (Intellectual)
- Is this team member experiencing a personal crisis? Is he or she going through a divorce? Is a child or family member in trouble? Is there a

financial hardship? Is this team member in conflict with a colleague or friend? (Emotional)
- Is this person experiencing an ethical crisis? Is the person involved in an unlawful matter? Is a value or belief changing and conflicting with the individual's values or life mission (career)? (Spiritual)

"Consider the possibility that a team member is habitually late not because he is disorganized or lazy, but perhaps because of an elderly parent who is sick. Or, perhaps a team member is late in completing a project. Instead of reprimanding the individual for poor job performance, ask the team member why the project is late. Is it late because of a physical reason? Is he sick? Is the project late because the individual moved out of his house due to a domestic reason? Is it late because of some other emergency that arose within his area of responsibility? Seek to understand the circumstances surrounding the issue at hand, in other words. Does this make sense to you?"

Billy said, "Yes, it does, Dr. Martin. Once, a colleague came to a staff meeting looking disheveled and forlorn. At the meeting's conclusion, he told me that he slept in his car the night before because he and his wife had an argument. He is the very example of which you speak. On that day, he could have been late in completing a project, possibly. His job performance was not at his ordinary level, understandably."

Katy said she could relate to Dr. Martin's admonition to examine one's condition. If she was tired or had a divided focus due to multiple issues before her, she tried not to make big decisions at that time. She usually would sleep on the matter before making a decision. Dr. Martin said, "These are two excellent examples. This intentional act of understanding self and others is not complicated. When leaders slow down and look at people, they can usually see that, in a number of cases, a struggle is taking place.

"When Solomon advised us to 'know the condition of our flocks,' imagine the shepherd who notices the sheep left behind. The unwise shepherd reprimands the animal with his staff without taking time to notice his condition. The wise shepherd examines his condition. Is he hurt? Why can't the animal keep up with the flock?"

2. DISPLAYING UNDERSTANDING THROUGH WORDS

Dr. Martin continued, "The wise leader models the Golden Rule. That is, he treats other people the way he wants to be treated. Before interacting with his team members collectively and individually, he asks himself, how he would want his supervisor to respond to him. The wise leader displays that he understands others by the manner in which he interacts with those entrusted to his supervision. He displays understanding through the careful use of words and actions. The wise leader listens, talks, and unselfishly gives his time and attention to support the individual.

"Remember that wise leaders possess Quality #5: self-control. The wise leader approaches situations with self-control when interacting with others. He is not easily offended; he is a patient leader who carefully chooses his words. He is not one to argue and he does not quickly speak. Solomon penned several proverbs related to this area. Look at the proverbs in the section, 'Displaying Understanding through Words,' on your handout. Katy, please read the first section."

Katy began reading the list of proverbs:

- Even a fool is thought wise if he keeps silent. —Proverbs 17:28
- A man of knowledge uses words with restraint. . . . —Proverbs 17:27
- He who guards his lips guards his life, but he who speaks rashly will come to ruin. —Proverbs 13:3
- He who guards his mouth and his tongue keeps himself from calamity. —Proverbs 21:23
- Do you see a man who speaks in haste? There is more hope for a fool than for him. —Proverbs 29:20
- It is to a man's honor to avoid strife, but every fool is quick to quarrel. —Proverbs 20:3

Billy said, "It is important to remain calm when addressing issues. And to be quiet and listen. In fact, it seems to me that Solomon is saying wise people listen more than they speak."

Katy agreed and said, "It is human nature to want to quickly weigh in on a matter when an issue is discussed. After reflecting on these proverbs, it is easy to see there is wisdom in using restraint when conveying one's thoughts."

Dr. Martin said, "That's right. Wise leaders remember that it is smart to use words carefully. My elementary teacher often reminded us: '*We have two ears and one mouth. Therefore, we should listen twice as much as we speak.*' And Solomon points out that there are dangerous words. Look at the next section of proverbs related to what I call 'flammable words' and 'healing words.' Billy, would you read the list?" Billy began to read the list aloud:

Flammable Words

- Do not pay attention to every word people say, or you may hear your servant cursing you—for you know in your heart that many times you yourself have cursed others. —Ecclesiastes 7:21–22

- Without wood a fire goes out; without gossip a quarrel dies down. —Proverbs 26:20
- A quarrelsome wife is like a constant dripping on a rainy day. —Proverbs 27:15
- Better to live on a corner of the roof than share a house with a quarrelsome wife. —Proverbs 25:24
- Do not boast about tomorrow. . . . —Proverbs 27:1
- Let someone else praise you, and not your own mouth; an outsider, and not your own lips. —Proverbs 27:2

Healing Words

- A gentle answer turns away wrath, but a harsh word stirs up anger. —Proverbs 15:1
- Do not withhold good from those who deserve it, when it is in your power to act. —Proverbs 3:27

Dr. Martin continued: "Thank you, Billy. As leaders listen to others, they watch out for flammable words they may hear *about themselves*. Solomon says don't pay attention to every word people say. Also, watch out for gossip about others. Don't repeat it. Don't be quarrelsome, or in other words, don't nag. Give correction in appropriate amounts. Don't provoke others. Solomon said it was better to live on the corner of the roof than to live with a quarrelsome wife. No one wants to be with an argumentative individual.

"Solomon cautions us not to boast about plans and accomplishments. He says people should let others praise them. His proverbs teach us that words can be healing. Wise leaders are gentle in their responses to others. They can and should seek gentle words, words of commendation, refreshing words. He also provides reminders for how and where time and attention is given."

3. DISPLAYING UNDERSTANDING THROUGH ACTIONS

"Silently read the proverbs in the next section: 'Displaying Understanding through Actions.'" Dr. Martin paused to give Katy and Billy time to reflect upon the proverbs.

Equal Time and Attention

- Seldom set foot in your neighbor's house—too much of you, and he will hate you. —Proverbs 25:17

No Partiality

- Do not gloat when your enemy falls. —Proverbs 24:17
- To show partiality in judging is not good. —Proverbs 24:23
- Speak up for those who cannot speak for themselves, for the rights of all who are destitute. Speak up and judge fairly; defend the rights of the poor and needy. —Proverbs 31:8–9
- He who gives to the poor will lack nothing, but he who closes his eyes to them receives many curses. —Proverbs 28:27

Dr. Martin said, "Are you careful about spending equal time with your team members? Do you intentionally seek time to plan or even have lunch with each of your team members periodically? Do you have favorites? Do you give a higher priority to people who are wealthy or powerful than those who are poor and needy? Solomon admonishes us to treat all people the same. And he expects us to speak up for those who cannot speak up for themselves. The king even warns us that those who ignore or close their eyes to the poor will receive many curses."

Katy said, "Wise leaders recognize that fairness is a fundamental value, and everyone must be treated the same regardless of background and socioeconomic level. Leaders must guard those entrusted to their care, and also represent the needy—those who cannot speak for themselves." Dr. Martin said, "You are fair and just. And, so are you, Billy."

4. A WORD OF CAUTION

"There is one final word of caution as this review of understanding others is completed: *Pick your battles carefully*. Once leaders examine the condition of their flocks, and respond to their needs, they must carefully examine the manner in which they can help those less fortunate. Look at the last section of proverbs listed on your handout. Solomon reminds us:

Pick Your Battles Carefully

- Like one who seizes a dog by the ears is a passer-by who meddles in a quarrel not his own. —Proverbs 26:17
- Do not speak to a fool, for he will scorn the wisdom of your words. —Proverbs 23:9

Katy understood the point Dr. Martin was making. Solomon was right. Leaders should not meddle in quarrels that are not their own. Their job is to listen and support the person, but not necessarily make the person's conflict their own conflict. Also, all people possess free will, and, as such, if a person will not listen and is foolish, leaders should not waste their time trying to help that person.

Billy said, "These two proverbs are true, and the wise will take heed in these situations. There was a conflict between two co-workers that escalated when the other employees took sides, and it divided the faculty and staff."

Katy said, "And, unfortunately, principals try unsuccessfully at times to reason with students about their poor choices when faced with disciplinary sanctions. After a period of time, teachers and principals have to try to help others who wish to be helped, as opposed to interacting with foolish people who simply will not listen."

Dr. Martin replied, "That's exactly right. Well stated."

Dr. Martin said, "In summary, leaders seek to understand others by staying calm in conflict. They treat others as they wish to be treated. Wise people look at the condition of their flocks through the PIES lenses. In interactions with others, leaders choose words carefully, recognizing that words can be flammable or healing. They don't have favorites. They treat all people the same and give equal time and attention to interactions. And finally, they pick their battles carefully and try not to take sides on issues of conflict.

"Now, for your final assignment: Identify a person that you respect because he or she seems to understand others. Write an essay about this person and the qualities the person possesses as they relate to the proverbs we discussed. Questions?"

Katy and Billy both shook their heads. They understood, and were already thinking about the people who surrounded them as they searched for a wise leader who possessed the gift of understanding. Katy said, "Thank you, Dr. Martin." She stood up to leave when Billy told her that he was learning layers upon layers of knowledge as he read Solomon's wise proverbs.

Billy thanked Dr. Martin for generating new ideas through Solomon's proverbs relating to supervision of others. He said, "Thank you, Dr. Martin, for sharing this time."

Dr. Martin said, "It is a pleasure to learn with you both and spend time reflecting upon wise leadership according to Solomon."

As Katy drove home, she thought about Cynthia Perkins, a person who exemplified the quality of understanding. She couldn't wait to get paper and pencil to outline the reasons she selected Ms. Perkins to be her example. Cynthia Perkins served as the school secretary at Independence High School. Cynthia is a wise leader who understands others, Katy thought. For more than fifteen years, Cynthia displayed this gift of understanding to the school's faculty, staff, students, and parents.

After supper, Katy easily prepared her outline and began to write the essay about Ms. Perkins. She opened her laptop and began to type:

Cynthia Perkins: A Wise Leader Who Understands Others

Cynthia Perkins, school secretary at Independence High School, is an example of a leader who possesses the gift of understanding. Ms. Perkins understands herself and she understands others. Cynthia exhibits the following qualities:

1. She exhibits self-control consistently.

2. She doesn't overreact because she is not easily offended.

3. She doesn't pay attention to every word that people say when they are upset.

4. She is an astute listener who chooses her words carefully.

5. She doesn't nag or brag.

6. She isn't afraid to speak up for the weak.

7. She refreshes others with healing words.

8. She shows no partiality—she treats each team member the same.

9. She never rejoices when a person who has been negative toward the school fails.

10. She remains neutral during times of conflict.

Cynthia works with parents, stakeholders, employees, and students. At times, because she is on the frontline, parents will be rude to her when they are emotionally charged about an event that occurred with their child at school or in the athletic arena. Because we work with children, the most treasured gift people have, emotions can run high at times and cause tempers to flair. Ms. Perkins never confuses emotions with personal attacks. She is not easily offended. She continues to treat others the way that she wants to be treated.

Cynthia may not be aware of the PIES lenses, but she does look at the physical, intellectual, emotional, and spiritual condition of people in her own way. Cynthia is socially literate. She is aware of body language. On more than one occasion, she can be heard quietly asking an employee, "How are you doing today?" when she notices a difference in the person's demeanor. Often, in a hushed voice, she will follow-up from a previous conversation with an employee to show her concern.

Cynthia has the unique ability to see trouble coming when visitors arrive by looking at the body language of the person before her. She can tell if the person is agitated, and she knows how to defuse the situation. For example, she will offer the person a cup of water or coffee and she will help to expedite the meeting between the person and the counselor or principal, if possible. She is watchful and knows when to call for assistance. She has good judgment and is an asset to our school because of the manner in which she interfaces with our stakeholders.

Also, Ms. Perkins knows when and how to give a "heads-up" at times because people trust her and share information with her. For example, a teacher recently told Cynthia about a negative Facebook post that a parent made about one of the coaches. Cynthia shared this information with me without attribution. This information was beneficial to me when I met with the parent because of the awareness her information provided.

Likewise, teachers and staff members trust her and often they will share confidences with her or express concerns about school business. Because of this trust, she, in turn, communicates concerns discreetly. For example, just last month a faculty meeting was rescheduled when she shared that many of our staff members were taking their children to the county fair that evening for a special concert. It didn't matter if the meeting was held on that particular day or one day during the next week, but it meant a lot to the teachers.

Ms. Perkins represents our school well. She is friendly, but always professional. She knows where the line is between friendly and professional. Cynthia Perkins is an astute listener. She is 100 percent there with whoever is in front of her. She carefully chooses her words. That is, she listens more than she speaks. Some employees are too friendly and they talk too much. Therefore, they struggle with task completion because of time management issues.

Ms. Perkins stays on task and minimizes conversations. A complaint has never been received about this gracious lady. It is amazing to watch her in action. Ms. Perkins is a safe spot for people. They can informally ask her questions about how to solve problems or share a burden with her.

Cynthia doesn't have favorites and she doesn't hold grudges. She doesn't take sides in times of conflict. She remains neutral. It has happened in schools where one person hated another person, and the team became divided. That is a most unpleasant situation for all. Cynthia says, "Today is a new day!" She truly believes this, and people know that they can approach her because she has no hidden agenda. She doesn't gossip or repeat confidential information.

Cynthia refreshes others. She displays a positive attitude and wears a smile on her face each day. She seems to notice when someone needs a word of encouragement. She can be heard sharing positive comments with team members. For example, last week Cynthia told a new teacher, Ms. Allen, that she was at church and overheard parents talking about what a good teacher she is and how their children were enjoying being in Ms. Allen's science class.

She was specific, too. Ms. Allen asked, "What in particular did they like?" Ms. Perkins said, "They talked about your enthusiasm, kindness, and knowledge of science." This conversation is in concert with the proverb in chapter 11, verse 25: "A generous man will prosper; he who refreshes others will himself be refreshed." I felt refreshed simply by hearing this positive exchange. Yes, Ms. Perkins is gracious and she refreshes others.

It is for these reasons and more that Ms. Cynthia Perkins represents the wise leader who possesses the quality of understanding. She is not easily offended. She chooses her words carefully. She refreshes others with her healing words. She has no favorites, and she remains neutral in times of conflict. It is a blessing to have the opportunity to work with this gracious leader. She is an inspiration to all who know her.

Katy proofed her essay and then attached it to her email to Dr. Martin:

Dr. Martin,

Attached please find my essay about Cynthia Perkins, a wonderful lady who possesses the gift of understanding. In the National Education Association's Code of Ethics, it states, "The educator, believing in the worth and dignity of each human being, recognizes the supreme importance of the pursuit of truth, devotion to excellence, and the nurture of the democratic principles." These proverbs speak truth to me each day. I am becoming a better leader by dwelling on them. Thank you.

—Katy

The next day, Katy received a reply from Dr. Martin:

Katy,

Thank you for your essay. I enjoyed reading it and I agree. Cynthia Perkins is an outstanding leader who understands others. She is a valuable asset to Independence High School and Washington County Schools. I also agree that Solomon's proverbs are truth. When we recognize truth, we start to see it in different arenas.

—R.M.

REFLECTION

That night, Katy opened her journal and formed reflective questions under the title "Quality #7: Wise Leaders Understand Others":

1. Why is it important to try to understand others?

2. How can a wise leader know the condition of his or her flock?

3. Explain the difference between flammable words and healing words.

4. How can I be a better listener?

5. Am I gracious in my interactions with others? Am I easily offended?

6. What does it mean to be socially literate? Am I socially literate?

7. Identify a leader who stands up for the poor and needy.

8. How does this person represent those who cannot represent themselves?

9. Am I an impartial leader? Do I show favoritism to friends or people of influence? Do I spend more time in one teacher's classroom or school or office than another?

10. *How does the quality of understanding others relate to national standards for educational leaders?*

Before she retired for the evening, she decided she wanted to "refresh" someone with healing words. She emailed Cynthia and attached a copy of her essay. She wrote:

Cynthia,

Oh, how I enjoy watching you work with others each day! You are a shining star in our school, and I am thankful for you. As you know, I am learning about leadership, according to Solomon, with Dr. Martin. He asked Billy Russell and me to identify and write an essay about a person who possesses the quality of understanding. I selected you. I thought you might like to read what I shared about you to our superintendent. See attached.

Thank you for your leadership. Thank you for your service to the IHS team. I am blessed to work with you.

With respect,

Katy

The next day, Katy found an email from Cynthia in her inbox. She thanked Katy for the kind email and essay about her. She wrote: "*Your timing is perfect, Dr. Carter. It has been a challenging month. As you know, my mother has been sick and it has been taxing due to multiple demands. Your kind email is encouraging. Thank you.*"

Katy told Cynthia when she came into the principal's office that she was sorry about her mother's illness. Katy added, "And every word in the essay is true." Cynthia had a tear in her eye as she quickly thanked Katy once more before she returned to the front office, where a parent was waiting for her attention.

The next week, Dr. Carter noticed a young woman's continued state of absenteeism as she reviewed the daily attendance report. She called her mother, who lamented about her condition and told the principal that she could not get her out of bed. The mother was exhausted and didn't know what to do. After considering the condition of her student through the PIES lenses, Dr. Carter boldly asked the mother if she could come to their house to see Melissa. The mother was appreciative and quickly replied, "Yes, that would be wonderful."

When Dr. Carter arrived, the mother went to Melissa's bedroom and told her of her principal's arrival. The fifteen-year-old girl came out to the living room shortly thereafter, a bit disheveled and slumped over. Dr. Carter motioned for Melissa to sit beside her on the sofa as Melissa's mother looked on from across the coffee table. Dr. Carter gently said, "Tell me why you don't want to come to school. You are greatly missed when you aren't at school."

Melissa's eyes filled with tears as she confided that she didn't have any friends at school, and she didn't like school.

Then she leaned over and put her head on the principal's shoulder and cried like a small child. The mother cried, too, as she came over and sat beside them, stroking her hair. Katy felt the pain of her student. She patted Melissa's shoulder as she wept and promised her they would find a better way for her at school. And that is exactly what happened.

Later that day, after Katy talked with Melissa and met with the school counselor, Melissa's schedule was amended so she could attend the Career Academy. Katy and the counselor also identified opportunities for Melissa to participate in clubs and volunteer in the community. They found a student in the mentoring program to befriend Melissa and invite her to eat with him at lunch.

Katy was pleased to incorporate Solomon's wisdom into her conferencing techniques. She was a better listener. She didn't "nag" Melissa about her attendance. Instead, she used healing words to encourage her to find the right pathway at school. And she spoke up for Melissa. She missed a deadline for some of her schoolwork and, as a result, she was failing English class.

Katy went with Melissa to meet with her teacher, and expressed confidence in her intellectual capacity. It was Melissa's battle, so she encouraged *her* to try to develop an agreement with this teacher so that she could complete and submit her work in order to earn credit. It worked out perfectly. Melissa was pleased because she successfully solved her own problem with little support. Her mother was happy to see Melissa on track with her education and career plans after high school.

Katy thought that Solomon was a wise king, indeed.

Conclusion

The Foolish, the Wicked, and the Wise

> The evil deeds of the wicked ensnare them. . . . For lack of discipline they will
> die, led astray by their own great folly. —Proverbs 5:22–23

Katy continued to weave Solomon's proverbs into her daily words and actions. As a result, this principal believed that the school team experienced
more success. The culture of the school seemed more caring, more equipped,
and more optimistic to Katy. And the individuals with whom she interacted
seemed happier with the outcomes. Leadership, according to Solomon, included vision, knowledge, ethics, humility, self-control, seeking counsel, and
understanding. Katy saw truth brilliantly shining within these seven qualities.
She was becoming a better leader because of this knowledge. She wanted to
incorporate these powerful leadership principles into school leadership
teams.

Using Solomon's wise advice to seek counsel, Katy called a meeting to
seek input from key leaders that included these individuals: school secretary,
student council president, teacher leader chair, and PTA president. Working
together, this planning committee developed plans for an event so that school
leaders could hear Dr. Martin speak about Solomon's leadership principles.
Filled with excitement, the planning team intended to make a memory for
their deserving school leaders. First, they needed to schedule a time for Dr.
Martin to speak.

Katy emailed Dr. Martin:

Dr. Martin,

Thank you for sharing the seven qualities of wise leadership, according to Solomon. As a result, positive results can be seen in my daily life, at school and at home. It's because of the awareness you created regarding the proverbs written by the wise king.

On behalf of the leadership team, you are invited to come to breakfast at Independence High School on Wednesday, February 20th at 7:00 a.m. in the Wendt Lecture Hall. Would it be possible for you to speak to our student, PTA, and school leaders about Solomon's leadership qualities at that time? Additionally, Ms. Martin is also invited to attend.

Thank you, sir.
With respect and appreciation,
Katy

Dr. Martin's secretary confirmed the superintendent's attendance and stated that Ms. Martin was delighted to be invited, and looked forward to attending as well. The planning team continued to work feverishly to create an epic big event. Dr. Carter liked to encourage others by using the popular phrase "Go Big or Go Home!"

The team divided tasks to be completed for the big event into six groups:

1. invitation/communication
2. food
3. decorations
4. take-aways for attendees (hand-out and memento)
5. order of program
6. thank you to Dr. Martin following the event

On Tuesday afternoon, the planning team met to prepare for the big event the next morning in the Wendt Lecture Hall—named after a master teacher who successfully served the students of Independence High School for forty-two years. The communication committee effectively distributed invitations to the event, and so secured confirmation that 134 leaders planned to attend. The Lecture Hall's seating capacity of 150 would be of sufficient size for the breakfast meeting. The guest list included a number of school leaders:

Student Council President and Officers
Head Custodian
Student Ambassadors
School Secretary
PTA President
PTA Officers and Committee Chairs
Lunchroom Manager
Teacher Leaders

Club Sponsors
Class Presidents
Club Presidents
Captains of athletic teams
Drum Major

Katy had not fully appreciated the multitude of leaders at Independence High School until that moment. Upon reviewing this influential and powerful list of leaders, this principal sadly realized missed opportunities. She should have called this group together long ago. A collector of quotes, Katy remembered one in particular that captured her sentiment at that moment: "*Alone we can do so little. Together we can do so much.*" A glass paperweight in Katy's office had these inspiring words of Helen Keller inscribed on its surface.

The food committee met with the lunchroom manager to plan the menu for the breakfast meeting. She and her team would prepare sausage and biscuits, fruit parfaits, and sweet rolls along with coffee, orange juice, and water. The three tables in the back of the room were covered down to the floor with beautiful black tablecloths that neatly stretched over the legs of the tables. The table in the center was adorned with the same black tablecloth, but it had a secondary white cloth that proudly displayed the gold crest of the school down its front. Napkins, cups, and plates, all in the school colors of crimson and blue, were arranged neatly on the tables.

The table decorations and programs communicated the theme of the meeting: leadership, according to Solomon. Each of Solomon's seven qualities of leadership was printed on the program along with an image:

1. Vision—eyeglasses
2. Knowledge—books
3. Ethics—a figure of Themis, the Greek goddess of justice
4. Humility—a figure of a man kneeling
5. Self-control—a printed card with the words "Yes or No" on it
6. Counsel—an image of an ear
7. Understanding—a light bulb

This program with the seven qualities was placed on each seat. They were ready.

The next morning, four of the Patriot Ambassadors were standing at the Independence High School's front doors to greet guests as they arrived. These outstanding students looked wonderful in their navy, khaki, and white attire. Each ambassador wore a professional gold magnetic badge with his or her name printed below the name of the school. To the left of the school name and the name of the ambassador, the crest of the school was displayed.

The ambassadors learned social skills in an induction class before they began their service. In it, they learned about grooming, body language, and manners. Each ambassador confidently greeted each guest by smiling and saying, "Good morning. Welcome to Independence High School." The ambassadors correctly wore their name badge above the pocket on the right side of their shirts or blazers so that it was easily visible during introductions and shaking of hands.

Liberty the Lion, the school's mascot, was in the commons area. He made people smile when they saw him. He embodied school spirit and community pride for IHS. The jazz band filled the school with energy with their cheerful tunes. As the band played, Liberty happily danced or made funny gestures.

After the ambassadors greeted the superintendent and his wife, Liberty walked over to them and shook hands with Dr. Martin. Then he kneeled before Ms. Martin and kissed her hand. Everyone laughed. Liberty the Lion then offered Ms. Martin his arm as he and two ambassadors escorted Dr. Martin and his wife to the lecture hall.

Dr. Martin wore khaki slacks with a blue-checked, oxford button down shirt and crimson pullover sweater vest. His signature bowtie was in place. Today, the bowtie he wore was gold. Covering navy argyle socks were his brown-suede saddle oxford shoes. Katy noticed an American flag lapel pin was properly placed on the left side of Dr. Martin's blazer—near his heart— as she walked over to welcome their special guests.

Ms. Martin was a quiet but friendly woman. She wore a simple navy dress with a white cashmere sweater jacket. Tucked inside the collar of the sweater was a beautiful gold silk scarf with small navy stars printed upon it. Peeking out from the scarf, a pearl necklace gently accented her attire. She wore classic, three-inch black leather pumps. One of the ambassadors presented a wrist corsage with miniature red roses to Ms. Martin when she arrived. Ms. Martin was deeply touched by this thoughtful gesture and immediately placed it on her wrist.

The breakfast food beautifully complemented the decorated tables. The aroma created by the hot coffee, fresh biscuits, and sweet rolls enticed the guests to join the line to select their favorite treats and beverage. Dr. and Ms. Martin enjoyed visiting with school leaders as they ate the delicious breakfast. A whisper developed into chatter as more and more of the leaders arrived. Soon the room was full of people, and the volume of chatter increased while the food decreased.

Without prompting, leaders selected seats and began reviewing the handout, found in each seat. Then Kermit, the student council president, walked to the podium and said, "Good morning. Please stand for the Pledge of Allegiance." Everyone recited the Pledge and returned to their seats.

Mack Howard, the junior class president, walked to the microphone next and said, "Welcome to our Special Leadership Breakfast Meeting. You are here today because you are a leader. Each person in this esteemed group represents a club, sport, or organization within our school. You have the opportunity to make a difference while you are serving in this leadership capacity at Independence High School. And you are encouraged to do so. Superintendent Martin and Ms. Martin, welcome to Independence High School, home of the Patriots. Dr. Martin will speak about leadership, according to Solomon. And now, Dr. Carter will introduce Dr. Martin."

Dr. Carter quickly walked to the podium and said, "Dr. Martin's favorite president, George Washington, said, '*I walk on untrodden ground. There is scarcely any part of my conduct which may not hereafter be drawn into precedent.*' Like our first president, the man for whom our county is named, people also watch you and your behavior. You are all role models. You are leaders and IHS is proud of each of you, whether you are a student or adult leader. You inspire others because of your leadership. The leaders in this room have one thing in common:

"*They seek to improve this wonderful school and the lives of its students, who walk the halls and learn in the classrooms of Independence High School.*"

Dr. Carter told the group that she wanted to become a better leader and a better person. During that year, she had the great fortune to learn about a stellar leader named Solomon from an outstanding leader named Dr. Ronnie Martin. She said, "Dr. Martin will talk to you about leadership, according to Solomon today. Ms. Martin, it is delightful to have you here today, also.

"Ladies and Gentlemen, let's give a rousing, Independence High School welcome to Superintendent Ronnie Martin!" The leaders stood up and clapped loudly, showing their appreciation and respect for Dr. Martin.

Dr. Martin walked with enthusiasm to the podium, smiled, and said, "Thank you, Dr. Carter. It is an honor to be here today. And it is a special treat to have Ms. Martin here as well." He paused for approximately ten to fifteen seconds. It seemed like an eternity, and all attendees were anxiously expecting his next words. He continued, "Raise your hand if you want to make the world a better place." All hands were raised in answer to the superintendent's directive. "Stand if you want to have a happy, successful life." Everyone in the room stood up.

Dr. Martin said, "Thank you. You may be seated. That's what I thought. Everyone in this room has a condition known as 'leader-itus.' Those with 'leader-itus' want to help others and make the world a better place. And they want to be successful in their personal lives as well. Everyone here today has it: *leader*-itus. Let's talk about how to be a successful leader, according to the wisest leader that ever lived. His name was Solomon, and he was a rich king.

"Solomon was the son of Israel's King David. His greatest accomplishment was building the Holy Temple in Jerusalem. When he became king in approximately 967 BC, according to the Bible, God told him he would give him anything he asked for, and Solomon asked for wisdom. He received the gift of wisdom and became the wisest man that ever lived. Solomon's name is synonymous with wisdom.

"He had much to say about life and he captured his ideas in the book of Proverbs, found in America's favorite book, the Bible. Solomon talks about three kinds of people in his writings:

1. the Foolish,
2. the Wicked, and
3. the Wise.

"The Foolish people are easy to identify. They hate discipline, and they bring grief to their parents. They know it all. They won't listen to those who try to help them get on the right path.

"The Wicked are known by their evil deeds. They are troublemakers who look for ways to harm others. They have no future. They often end up in jail or do not live a long life. And then there are the Wise. Wise people bring joy to their parents. They are seekers of continual improvement. They are eager to learn. They want to help others and they want to be successful. If you are seated in this room today, then you are in the group of people who desire wisdom.

"There are seven qualities that wise, enduring, successful leaders possess. Solomon wrote about these qualities. Now, before you learn about the seven qualities that wise leaders possess, there is a secret to be shared." Dr. Martin walked toward the leaders and whispered, "This speaker before you now is not an expert on any of this information. He is a learner, just as you are learners."

In a normal voice he said, "It seems, through studying Solomon's proverbs and through my observations of others, that there are seven qualities that wise leaders have in their personal and professional lives: Vision, Knowledge, Ethics, Humility, Self-Control, Counsel, and Understanding."

Students and adults were intently listening to Dr. Martin. Some had a pen in hand to take notes on the provided handout. Others were using their smartphone to capture ideas. And Dr. Martin mesmerized numerous leaders with his wise words; they sat and listened with their full attention. Dr. Martin said, "As each quality is reviewed, a proverb will be read from King Solomon that relates to it, and questions will be posed for reflection.

Quality #1: Wise Leaders Are *Visionary*
Where there is no vision, the people perish. —Proverbs 29:18
Do you know a visionary leader? Do you plan for the future? Do you think about the days to come?

Quality #2: Wise Leaders Are *Seekers of Knowledge*
Pay attention and listen to the sayings of the wise. —Proverbs 22:17
Are you a lifelong learner? Are you observant? Watchful? Do you study and value education?

Quality #3: Wise Leaders Are *Ethical*
By justice a king gives a country stability. —Proverbs 29:4
Are you a person of character? Do you treat others with fairness? Are you impartial or do you have favorites? Do you obey the rules? Laws? Are you a role model?

Quality #4: Wise Leaders Are *Humble*
When pride comes, then comes disgrace, but with humility comes wisdom. —Proverbs 11:2
Do you want the credit when good happens? Do you consider others better than yourself? Are you arrogant? Prideful?

Quality #5: Wise Leaders Are *Self-Controlled*
A fool gives full vent to his anger, but a wise man keeps himself under control. —Proverbs 29:11
Do you control your temper? Are you in control of alcohol, food, and sexual behavior? Do you have a good work ethic? Are you easily offended? Do you carefully choose your friends?

Quality #6: Wise Leaders *Seek Counsel*
Plans fail for lack of counsel, but with many advisors they succeed. —Proverbs 15:22
Do you welcome advice? Do you seek input from others? Do you welcome discipline or correction from your parents, teachers, and supervisors, or do you hate it?

Quality #7: Wise Leaders *Understand Others*
Be sure you know the condition of your flocks. . . . —Proverbs 27:23
Do you know your friends' condition? Do you heal them with your words or do you injure them with your words? Are you quick to quarrel or slow to speak? Do you gossip or brag? Do you speak up for the poor and needy or are you partial to your friends? Do you pick your battles carefully or are you swayed to defend the causes your friends identify?

"Friends, Solomon's proverbs are overflowing with wise advice for all types of people. His wisdom is for the foolish, the wicked, and the wise. But the foolish reject it. And the wicked don't want it because they enjoy hurting others, including themselves. But the wise eagerly accept Solomon's advice. The wise listen and learn.

"Ask yourself today if you are a wise leader. Do you possess the seven qualities Solomon speaks of in his proverbs? Are you visionary? Do you seek knowledge? Are you ethical? Are you humble? Do you possess self-control? Do you seek counsel? Do you understand yourself and others?

"If the answer to all of these questions is yes, then you are a wise leader, or you are becoming a wise leader. Wise leaders strive to possess these seven leadership qualities, according to Solomon. Your superintendent wants to be in that group of people—the wise. He wants to associate with wise people. Solomon said in Proverbs 13:20, *'He who walks with the wise grows wise, but a companion of fools suffers harm.'*

"Solomon said in Proverbs 4:7–9, *'Wisdom is supreme; therefore get wisdom. Though it cost all you have, get understanding. Esteem her, and she will exalt you; embrace her, and she will honor you. She will set a garland of grace on your head and present you with a crown of splendor.'*

"Solomon also said in Ecclesiastes 2:13–14, *'I saw that wisdom is better than folly, just as light is better than darkness. The wise man has eyes in his head, while the fool walks in the darkness.'*

"Solomon had chilling words for the foolish and wicked. In Proverbs 5:11–14 he said to them, *'At the end of your life you will groan, when your flesh and body are spent. You will say, "How I hated discipline! How my heart spurned correction! I would not obey my teachers or turn my ear to my instructors. And I was soon in serious trouble in the Assembly of God's people."'* And in verses 22–23, he said, *'The evil deeds of the wicked ensnare them; the cords of their sins hold them fast. For lack of discipline they will die, led astray by their own great folly.'*

"Thank you, Dr. Carter, for inviting me to speak to you all today about leadership, according to Solomon." Student and adult leaders sprang to their feet to give Dr. Martin a standing ovation. They clapped their hands loudly. Dr. Martin started to walk off the stage when Dr. Carter stopped him as she joined him on the stage.

Katy said, "Dr. Martin, thank you for being here today. Solomon's lessons about wise leadership will be long remembered." Several others joined them on the stage. Each one of them stepped up to the microphone as soon as one completed his sentence. Together, the group formed the following message, one sentence at a time:

"Dr. Martin, in honor of your dedication and commitment to education, we name you as the founding member of a new club—the Kings Club, named after the wise King Solomon."

"The Kings Club begins today at Independence High School. It is a club for class presidents and club presidents, and all leaders who wish to become wise leaders."

"The Kings Club is based on the seven qualities that wise leaders possess, according to King Solomon: vision, knowledge, ethics, humility, self-control, counsel, and understanding."

"The very first Kings Club lapel pin is presented to you today, Dr. Martin."

The last student to speak shook hands with Dr. Martin as she presented the gold pin to him. It was 1.5 inches wide and 1.0 inch tall. The pin was a gold crown with seven jewels. Inscribed on the pin was "Kings Club." Each of the jewels had one of the seven qualities inscribed below it. Dr. Martin pinned the Kings Club crown on his lapel. His eyes were filled with tears as he realized that Solomon's powerful, wise admonitions would be shared with student leaders not only today, but in the years to come.

The class president walked up to the microphone and said, "Dr. Martin, thank you for caring about us. Thank you, sir." Dr. Martin shook his hand.

Dr. Carter returned to the microphone and said, "There is a Kings Club lapel pin for each of you. Please come to the stage as guided by the ambassadors to receive your pin. Dr. Martin, will you assist me in distributing the pins?" He nodded his head and humbly stood beside the principal. After she distributed a beautiful pin to each leader, he shook hands with each attendee.

Kings Club Lapel Pin.

AFTER THE MEETING

It was 8:00 a.m. The students were now in class along with their teacher leaders. The PTA president, Jan Ingram, and the officers stayed to help clean up after the breakfast. Katy escorted Dr. Martin and his wife to the front door of the school. He thanked Katy for the opportunity to be part of the big event. Katy thanked him for mentoring her and teaching her about wise leadership, according to Solomon. He would never know how much she appreciated his life-changing guidance.

Dr. Martin smiled and told her the pleasure was all his. He told Katy that she covered mentoring others today in a big way. He would never forget it. Ms. Martin was grateful to be present to witness her husband's leadership come to life in the form of a school club—the Kings Club.

Katy handed Dr. Martin an envelope. On the front it read, "To John and Mary, the children of Dr. and Ms. Ronnie Martin." Katy said, "This is a gift to your children."

Dr. Martin seemed a bit puzzled, but smiled and simply said, "Thank you." Ms. Martin smiled and said good-bye.

That night, Katy penned the following questions in her journal:

Conclusion: The Foolish, the Wicked and the Wise

a. What are the three types of people described by Solomon?
b. How can we identify a foolish person?
c. How can we identify a wicked person?
d. What qualities do the Wise possess?
e. How do I seek wisdom in my leadership role?

At the Martin home that night at supper, Ms. Martin opened Katy's letter and began to read it to their two children:

Dear John and Mary,
I work for your father. My name is Katy and I am one of the principals that your father supervises. I want to tell you about your father and the kind of leader he is in the workplace.
Your father, Dr. Ronnie Martin, is a visionary leader who plans for the future. We feel secure knowing that Dr. Martin is in charge of our school district. He is competent because he continually studies and seeks knowledge. He is an outstanding leader who is a man of character. He is honest and kind, and he speaks up for the weak and poor.
Your father is patient with his employees. He never holds a grudge when we make mistakes. He is self-disciplined in all areas of his life, and because

of this, he is an inspiration to all who know him. He makes us feel important at work. He often asks our opinion about new ideas or improvement efforts.

Dr. Martin understands us. He uses refreshing words of encouragement when we make mistakes or if we are feeling low. He speaks very little at work, but when he speaks you better listen, because whatever he says will be worth hearing.

I wanted to write you this letter to tell you that there are lots of people who think your father is a wonderful leader, and I am only one of them.

With respect,

Katy Carter

Principal, Independence High School

Because she was deeply touched, Ms. Martin cried as she read the beautiful words about her husband to her children. She framed the letter and hung it on the wall in the children's playroom so they could read it again and again through the years to come. She hoped that John and Mary would grow up and become like their wise father, in all the ways that Katy Carter so eloquently described.

Epilogue

It was April when Katy received the job announcement. The superintendent's position was open in the adjoining county. Dr. Wilson was retiring in July. The position would be posted for two months. Interviews were to be conducted during the first week of June.

Katy cautiously tucked the printed job posting in her satchel. She looked forward to sharing it with Daniel. Should she apply? Was she ready? After supper that night, Katy and Daniel went for a long walk. Katy said, "You will never guess what Dr. Martin sent to my inbox today—a job posting for superintendent of Lincoln County."

Daniel stopped walking and turned to look at Katy. He grinned as he gave her a big hug. "Go for it, Katy. You're ready for this. You would be an excellent superintendent." Katy smiled.

Dr. Kathleen Estelle Olive Carter was destined to become a teacher. And she taught mathematics. Then she became a principal. She treasured the time she spent teaching her beautiful students and then serving as their principal. Now, she optimistically looked to future days of possibly serving as a school district's superintendent.

Katy would indeed apply for this outstanding opportunity. She started thinking about all the details of applying for the position as they walked, hand in hand, toward the setting sun.

The End

Appendix A:
Webster's Dictionary of Terms

Counsel—advice given

Discernment—the ability to see and understand people, things, or situations clearly and intelligently

Ethics—a set of moral principles

Evil—morally bad; causing harm or injury to someone

Fool—a person who lacks good sense or judgment; a stupid or silly person

Humility—freedom from pride or arrogance

Instruction—a statement that describes how to do something; the action or process of teaching

Knowledge—information, understanding, or skill that you get from experience or education

Leader—a person who has commanding authority or influence

Proverb—a general truth, fundamental principle, or rule of conduct

Seek—to go in search of; look for

Self-control—restraint exercised over one's own impulses, emotions, or desires

Solomon—son of David and 10th century BC king of Israel proverbial for his wisdom

Teacher—one whose occupation is to instruct

Understanding—the knowledge and ability to judge a particular situation or subject

Vision—unusual discernment or foresight

Wicked—morally bad

Wisdom—knowledge of what is proper or reasonable; good sense or judgment

Appendix B: Proverbs Related to Seven Qualities

"The proverbs of Solomon, son of David, king of Israel: for attaining wisdom and discipline; for understanding and words of insight; for acquiring a disciplined and prudent life, doing what is right and just and fair." (Proverbs 1:1–3)

1. VISIONARY

- Where there is no vision, the people perish. —Proverbs 29:18

2. SEEKERS OF KNOWLEDGE

- Pay attention and listen to the sayings of the wise. —Proverbs 22:17
- The wise store up knowledge, but the mouth of a fool invites ruin. —Proverbs 10:14
- I, wisdom, dwell together with prudence; I possess knowledge and discretion. —Proverbs 8:12
- The prudent see danger and take refuge. —Proverbs 27:12
- A man who remains stiff-necked after many rebukes will suddenly be destroyed—without remedy. —Proverbs 29:1

3. ETHICAL

- By justice a king gives a country stability, but those who are greedy for bribes tear it down. —Proverbs 29:4

- The proverbs of Solomon son of David, king of Israel: for gaining wisdom and instruction; for understanding words of insight; for receiving instruction in prudent behavior, *doing what is right and just and fair.* —Proverbs 1:1–3
- The wicked flee though no one pursues, but the righteous are as bold as a lion. —Proverbs 28:1
- To show partiality is not good—yet a person will do wrong for a piece of bread. —Proverbs 28:21
- Those who give to the poor will lack nothing, but those who close their eyes to them receive many curses. —Proverbs 28:27
- If a king judges the poor with fairness, his throne will be established forever. —Proverbs 29:14
- Speak up for those who cannot speak for themselves, for the rights of all who are destitute. Speak up and judge fairly; defend the rights of the poor and needy. —Proverbs 31:8–9

4. HUMBLE

- When pride comes, then comes disgrace, but with humility comes wisdom. —Proverbs 11:2
- A man's pride will bring him low, but a humble spirit will obtain honor. —Proverbs 29:23, NASB
- Do not be wise in your own eyes. —Proverbs 3:7
- Do you see a man wise in his own eyes? There is more hope for a fool than him. —Proverbs 26:12
- Let someone else praise you, and not your own mouth; an outsider, and not your own lips. —Proverbs 27:2
- The crucible for silver and the furnace for gold, but people are tested by their praise. —Proverbs 27:21
- Do not exalt yourself in the king's presence, and do not claim a place among great men; it is better for him to say to you, "Come up here," than for him to humiliate you before a nobleman. —Proverbs 25:6–7

5. SELF-CONTROLLED

Anger

- A fool gives full vent to his anger, but a wise man keeps himself under control. —Proverbs 29:11

Food (Gluttony)

• Do not join those who drink too much wine, or gorge themselves on meat, for drunkards and gluttons become poor. . . . —Proverbs 23:20–21

Alcohol

• It is not for kings to drink wine, not for rulers to crave beer, lest they drink and forget what has been decreed, and deprive all the oppressed of their rights. —Proverbs 31:4–5

Work Ethic

• Lazy hands make for poverty, but diligent hands bring wealth. —Proverbs 10:4
• A little sleep, a little slumber, a little folding of the hands to rest—and poverty will come on you like a thief. . . . —Proverbs 24:33–34

Sexual Behavior

• A man who commits adultery lacks judgment. —Proverbs 6:32

Stability

• If you fall to pieces in a crisis, there wasn't much to you in the first place. —Proverbs 24:10, MSG

Answering a Foolish Person

• Do not answer a fool according to his folly, or you will be like him yourself. —Proverbs 26:4

Patience

• A person's wisdom yields patience. . . . —Proverbs 19:11
• Better a patient man than a warrior, a man who controls his temper than one who takes a city. —Proverbs 16:32

Not Easily Offended

• It is to one's glory to overlook an offense. —Proverbs 19:11

Choosing Friends

- Do not make friends with a hot-tempered man, do not associate with one easily angered, or you may learn his ways and get yourself ensnared. —Proverbs 22:24–25

6. SEEK COUNSEL

- Plans fail for lack of counsel, but with many advisors they succeed. —Proverbs 15:22
- Wounds from a friend can be trusted. —Proverbs 27:6
- An honest answer is like a kiss on the lips. —Proverbs 24:26
- He who ignores discipline comes to poverty and shame, but whoever heeds correction is honored. —Proverbs 13:8
- As iron sharpens iron, so one man sharpens another. —Proverbs 27:17
- Wisdom is found in those who take advice. —Proverbs 13:10
- A fool spurns his father's discipline, but whoever heeds correction shows prudence. —Proverbs 15:5
- Whoever loves discipline loves knowledge; but he who hates correction is stupid. —Proverbs 12:1
- It is better to heed a wise man's rebuke than to listen to a song of fools. —Ecclesiastes 7:5
- For lack of guidance a nation falls, but victory is won through many advisers. —Proverbs 11:14
- The way of fools seems right to them, but the wise listen to advice. —Proverbs 12:15

7. UNDERSTANDING

- Be sure you know the condition of your flocks. . . . —Proverbs 27:23

Self-Control

- A hot-tempered man stirs up dissension, but a patient man calms a quarrel. —Proverbs 15:18
- A man's wisdom gives him patience; it is to his glory to overlook an offense. —Proverbs 19:11

Careful Use of Words

- Even a fool is thought wise if he keeps silent. —Proverbs 17:28
- A man of knowledge uses words with restraint. . . . —Proverbs 17:27

- He who guards his lips guards his life, but he who speaks rashly will come to ruin. —Proverbs 13:3
- He who guards his mouth and his tongue keeps himself from calamity. —Proverbs 21:23
- It is to a man's honor to avoid strife, but every fool is quick to quarrel. —Proverbs 20:3
- Do you see a man who speaks in haste? There is more hope for a fool than for him. —Proverbs 29:20

Flammable Words

- Do not pay attention to every word people say, or you may hear your servant cursing you—for you know in your heart that many times you yourself have cursed others. —Ecclesiastes 7:21–22
- Without wood a fire goes out; without gossip a quarrel dies down. —Proverbs 26:20
- Do not slander a servant to his master, or he will curse you, and you will pay for it. —Proverbs 30:10
- A quarrelsome wife is like a constant dripping on a rainy day. —Proverbs 27:15
- Better to live on a corner of the roof than share a house with a quarrelsome wife. —Proverbs 25:24
- Do you see a man who speaks in haste? There is more hope for a fool than for him. —Proverbs 29:20
- Do not boast about tomorrow. . . . —Proverbs 27:1
- Let someone else praise you, and not your own mouth; an outsider, and not your own lips. —Proverbs 27:2

Healing Words

- A gentle answer turns away wrath, but a harsh word stirs up anger. —Proverbs 15:1
- Do not withhold good from those who deserve it, when it is in your power to act. —Proverbs 3:27
- A generous man will prosper; he who refreshes others will himself be refreshed. —Proverbs 11:25

Equal Time and Attention

- Seldom set foot in your neighbor's house—too much of you, and he will hate you. —Proverbs 25:17

No Partiality

- Do not gloat when your enemy falls. —Proverbs 24:17
- To show partiality in judging is not good. —Proverbs 24:23
- Speak up for those who cannot speak for themselves, for the rights of all who are destitute. Speak up and judge fairly; defend the rights of the poor and needy. —Proverbs 31:8–9
- He who gives to the poor will lack nothing, but he who closes his eyes to them receives many curses. —Proverbs 28:27

Pick Your Battles Carefully

- Like one who seizes a dog by the ears is a passer-by who meddles in a quarrel not his own. —Proverbs 26:17
- Do not speak to a fool, for he will scorn the wisdom of your words. —Proverbs 23:9

CONCLUSION: THE FOOLISH, THE WICKED AND THE WISE

The Foolish

- Fools despise wisdom and discipline. —Proverbs 1:7
- A wise son brings joy to his father, but a foolish son brings grief to his mother. —Proverbs 10:1
- He who walks with the wise grows wise, but a companion of fools suffers harm. —Proverbs 13:20
- Why should fools have money in hand to buy wisdom, when they are not able to understand it? Proverbs 17:16

The Wicked

- The evil deeds of the wicked ensnare them; the cords of their sins hold them fast. For lack of discipline they will die. —Proverbs 5:22–23
- A scoundrel plots evil, and on their lips it is like a scorching fire. —Proverbs 16:27
- The wicked crave evil; their neighbors get no mercy from them. —Proverbs 21:10
- . . . for the evildoer has no future hope, and the lamp of the wicked will be snuffed out. —Proverbs 24:20
- At the end of your life you will groan, when your flesh and body are spent. You will say, "How I hated discipline! How my heart spurned correction! I would not obey my teachers or turn my ear to my instructors, and I was

soon in serious trouble in the assembly of God's people." —Proverbs 5:11–14

The Wise

- Wisdom is supreme; therefore get wisdom. Though it cost all you have, get understanding. Esteem her, and she will exalt you; embrace her, and she will honor you. She will set a garland of grace on your head and present you with a crown of splendor. —Proverbs 4:7–9
- Above all else, guard your heart, for it is the wellspring of life. Put away perversity from your mouth; keep corrupt talk far from your lips. Let your eyes look straight ahead, fix your gaze directly before you. Make level paths for your feet and take only ways that are firm. Do not swerve to the right or the left; keep your foot from evil. —Proverbs 4: 23–27
- I saw that wisdom is better than folly, just as light is better than darkness. —Ecclesiastes 2:13
- The wise man has eyes in his head, while the fool walks in the darkness. —Ecclesiastes 2:14

Appendix C: Reflective Questions

1. What is the purpose of having a mentor?
2. What assignment did Katy's mentor give her?
3. What is the job description for a leader?
4. How does one become an enduring, successful superintendent or leader?
5. Solomon

    a. Who was Solomon?
    b. How did he become wise?
    c. Where can his writings be found?
    d. What is an example of his wise leadership and decision-making?

6. Quality #1: Wise Leaders Are Visionary

    a. What is visionary leadership?
    b. Billy Coleman is an example of a visionary leader in this book. Do you know a visionary leader?
    c. What did this person do to become a visionary leader?
    d. How does this proverb relate to educational leadership standards?

7. Quality #2: Wise Leaders Are Seekers of Knowledge

    a. What does it mean to be a seeker of knowledge?
    b. What lesson can you learn from the example of Dr. Barry Carroll?

   c. Name a leader you know that is a seeker of knowledge.

   d. How can you be a lifelong learner?

   e. How does seeking knowledge relate to national standards for educational leaders?

8. Quality #3: Wise Leaders Are Ethical

   a. Identify a leader who stands up for the poor and needy.

   b. How does this person represent those who cannot represent themselves?

   c. Are you an impartial leader? Do you show favoritism to students, friends, or people of influence? Do you spend more time in one teacher's classroom or school or office than another's?

   d. How do Solomon's proverbs relate to professional educational leadership standards in your state or at the national level?

9. Quality #4: Wise Leaders Are Humble

   a. Identify a leader that possesses humility.

   b. What qualities does this humble leader consistently exhibit?

   c. How do you demonstrate that you value others? Do you seek their input?

   d. Are you totally engaged with others as they speak to you? Do you listen more than you speak?

   e. List three ways you can be a more humble leader.

   f. Do you consider others to be more important than yourself?

10. Quality #5: Wise Leaders Are Self-Controlled

   a. What are the two groups of proverbs related to self-control?

   b. List the five themes from the two groups related to self-control.

   c. From headlines in the news, find and list three examples of educational leaders who did not exhibit self-control.

   d. List three to five proverbs that help you remember the importance of self-control not only with self, but also with others.

11. Quality #6: Wise Leaders Seek Counsel

a. Identify one person who seeks counsel. How/why did this person seek correction/input?
b. Have you ever sought input or advice from others in order to make a plan for improvement?
c. If so, how did you seek their advice? Face-to-face meeting? Survey? Email?
d. How did Dr. Spivey incorporate the advice she received into her plan for applying for superintendent?

12. Quality #7: Wise Leaders Understand Others

a. Why is it important to try to understand others?
b. How can a wise leader know the condition of his or her flock?
c. Explain the difference between flammable words and healing words.
d. How can you be a better listener?
e. Are you gracious in your interactions with others? Are you easily offended?
f. What does it mean to be socially literate? Are you socially literate?
g. Identify a leader who stands up for the poor and needy.
h. How does this person represent those who cannot represent themselves?
i. Are you an impartial leader? Do you show favoritism to friends or people of influence? Do you spend more time in one teacher's classroom or school or office than another's?
j. How does the quality of understanding others relate to national standards for educational leaders?

13. Conclusion: The Foolish, the Wicked and the Wise

a. What are the three types of people described by Solomon?
b. How can we identify a foolish person?
c. How can we identify a wicked person?
d. What qualities do the wise possess?
e. How do you seek wisdom in your leadership role?

Appendix D: Excerpt from Dr. Spivey's Portfolio

Sandra W. Spivey, EdD
Candidate for Superintendent of the Scottsboro City School System

TABLE OF CONTENTS

Section 1:

- Letter to School Board Members
- Resume
- Professional Certificates

Section 2:

- Growing Up in Scottsboro
- Faith and Family
- Christmas Cards

Section 3:

- Phenix City School System

  1. Math Teacher and Cheerleading Sponsor at Central High School

Section 4:

- Alexander City School System

    1. Math Teacher, Cheerleading Coach, and Extracurricular Bus Driver at Benjamin Russell High School
    2. Assistant Principal at Benjamin Russell High School
    3. Acting Principal/Principal at Alexander City Middle School
    4. Principal at Benjamin Russell High School

- Newspaper Article
- Highlights from 2004–2005 at BRHS
- Letter of Recommendation

Section 5:

- Hoover City School System

    1. Principal at Hoover High School
    2. Director of Human Resources, Central Office

- Letters of Recommendation

Section 6:

- Madison County School System

    1. Director of Secondary Education

- *High School Academic Guide and Course Catalog (2014–2015)*
- *Athletics Guide, 2014–2015*
- *Framework for Excellence* and *Framework of Excellence*
- Letters of Recommendation
- Partnership with Samford University and EXCEL21 Leadership Academy
- Letter of Recommendation
- *Leadership Huntsville/Madison County*

Section 7:

- Alabama State Department of Education

    1. Regional Support Coordinator for Regions 3 & 5

- Letter of Recommendation

Section 8:

- What You Can Expect from Me if I Am Selected to Be the Next Superintendent in the Scottsboro City School System

    1. Communication
    2. Community
    3. Leadership
    4. Superintendent and School Board Relationships
    5. Fiscal Management
    6. Human Resources
    7. Safety
    8. Technology
    9. Co-Curricular Activities
    10. Fine Arts
    11. Athletics
    12. Career and Technical Education
    13. Special Education, etc.
    14. Plan 2020
    15. Accountability
    16. Ninety-Day Plan of Action
    17. My Commitment to You

WHAT YOU CAN EXPECT FROM ME IF I AM SELECTED TO BE THE NEXT SUPERINTENDENT IN THE SCOTTSBORO CITY SCHOOL SYSTEM

Communication

Establishing relationships based on trust, candor, and respect is critical, and effective communication and engagement is very important in developing these relationships. I would work with the school board members and our system's/school's leadership team to develop and implement a strategic plan for communicating information to our stakeholders and expand the tools we use in those efforts. It is important to be intentional and organized in an effort to engage the community in a partnership, in which there are opportunities for us to share information as well as to listen.

Community

I believe citizens are a valuable resource, and we should seek out their ideas, listen to their opinions, and find opportunities to use their talents. I think it is important to be very deliberate in keeping the citizens informed about school system activities, achievements, and needs instead of leaving it to chance, and it is important to include in the plan opportunities for citizens to provide input in ways that make sense for the school system. A positive climate for all employees is important, and, in establishing a positive climate, communication is critical. Again, I think it goes back to trust, candor, and respect. If any one of these three is compromised, the working environment is jeopardized, and this gets "passed down" to the students and into the community.

Leadership

As a superintendent, keeping a positive attitude is important. I believe the rest of the organization "feeds" off of the attitude of the leader. An important aspect of the climate is remembering that we are all here to serve. If we keep a service mentality, whether it's the teacher, the custodian, the secretary, the principal, or the superintendent, and if everything we say and do reflects an attitude of service, there will be a positive climate. It starts at the top.

When big decisions have to be made, I have always been able to work with the appropriate group of people to reach consensus. I don't just sit in my office coming up with rules/guidelines for others to follow; everybody has input, and we work together to find the best solution to any problem that arises. I like to deal with problems directly. When I have a concern or question, I do not hesitate to talk to the appropriate people about it. I try to address problems as quickly as possible when they arise so they do not grow. The people I directly supervise have all been comfortable calling me when they have questions/concerns. I think they have found that I am pretty much "on call" most of the time, day or night, and I stand ready to try to assist them as best I can when problems arise or when they are trying to think ahead and be seekers of knowledge in preventing problems or implementing new programs/procedures.

Superintendent and School Board Relationships

The superintendent and school board members are important leaders in the community who are charged with the specific responsibility of creating a quality school system for students. Although each has a specific role, they must work together to solve problems and to set and attain common goals. In broad terms, policy-making is the responsibility of the board, and administration is the responsibility of the superintendent and staff. However, the superintendent should work with the board as a unified body whose greatest concern is the educational welfare of the students attending the schools. As a superintendent, I would do the following to create an effective partnership with the board:

- *Ensure that board members are kept fully informed about the general state of the schools and the issues affecting operations;*
- *Work with the school board and other stakeholders to develop goals for our system;*
- *Work with board members to plan and conduct productive board meetings in which board members, as well as the appropriate staff members, have the necessary information in order to make the best decisions; and*
- *Most importantly, since the superintendent and board set the tone and direction for the system, I would work very hard to establish a true partnership with the board in which there is trust, candor, and respect.*

Fiscal Management

Regarding fiscal management, in my view, the superintendent must work closely with the CSFO and school board to develop, adopt, and monitor an annual budget and to ensure that the school system is financially sound, adheres to its budget, and follows proper financial procedures. The superintendent and CSFO must work closely with the directors/coordinators and principals/bookkeepers to establish budgets and monitor accounts. The superintendent and CSFO must work together to make sure all employees have the information they need in their areas of responsibility to follow financial policies/procedures, and they must work together, along with the appropriate system-level staff members, to hold everyone accountable and address any problems that may arise. Once a strategic plan is developed, it is important to work to make sure top priorities in the plan are reflected in the budget. Where only short-term funding is available in certain areas, there must be diligence in looking at long-term sustainability before accepting funds and agreeing to implement programs. I feel a responsibility that those who make an investment in the school system feel that it is a good one. Communication is critical in this area, in my opinion. The more I have gotten involved in the greater community, the more I realize there is a general lack of understanding with most stakeholders regarding school/system finances; therefore, we must be deliberate in communicating our message and engaging the community in this conversation.

Human Resources

Recruiting, retaining, and developing excellent employees are critical to creating and sustaining a high-quality school system. Here are my thoughts regarding each of these areas:

- *Recruiting employees:*

    -Encourage and prepare future/aspiring teachers (TEACH Alabama, FEA, etc.)
    -Seek out the "best and brightest"
    -Create and maintain an excellent school system (the best recruiting tool)

- *Retaining employees:*

    -Monitor employee data (e.g., when people leave, why are they leaving?)
    -Support employees by making sure they have the tools they need to succeed (e.g., put them in a position to "win")
    -Treat employees fairly and with respect
    -Celebrate accomplishments/achievements
    -Make expectations clear
    -Continue to be an excellent school system (the best retention tool)

- *Developing employees:*

    -Support employees by making sure they have the tools they need to succeed (e.g., put them in a position to "win")
    -Provide appropriate professional development and ongoing support
    -Give employees the opportunity to "shine" and lead
    As the superintendent, it would be my responsibility to model servant leadership and provide ongoing support and encouragement to all employees.

Safety

One of the most important roles of the superintendent is to make sure to cultivate a disciplined and safe school environment for students, faculty, and staff. The following are important in creating and sustaining a disciplined/ safe environment:

- *Establish fair/clear guidelines and clearly communicate expectations;*
- *Treat people with dignity and respect, but be firm regarding expectations;*
- *Apply the principles of the "Leader in Me" program: (1) be seekers of knowledge, (2) begin with the end in mind, (3) put first things first, (4)*

think win-win, (5) seek first to understand, then to be understood, (6) synergize, and (7) sharpen the saw;

- *Review plans/policies/procedures on a regular basis and make needed changes;*
- *Assess facilities/equipment (in partnership with other local agencies) and address areas of concern; and*
- *Provide training for employees and students regarding emergency situations.*

Technology

Technology is a very important part of the educational process.
My background regarding technology is summarized below:

- *Things have changed a lot since I graduated from Auburn University in 1990, when I was trained in the old programming/DOS systems, and even since I earned my doctorate in 2004.*
- *I participated in the Superintendents' Academy in 2010, and one of the sessions was entitled "A Shared Vision for Technology—The Superintendent's Role." Topics included the following: AETC Conference; Ensuring Educators Move from Technology Training to Implementation through Effective Training and Support; How to Fund Technology and Libraries by Leveraging Other Funding Sources; Data Integration and Decision-Making; Cyberbullying, Social Networking, and Internet Crimes; and Laptops vs. iPads.*
- *I was fortunate to attend the ISTE (International Society for Technology in Education) conference while I was in Madison County, and I attended many sessions designed specifically for administrators.*
- *I have participated in many professional development opportunities focused on technology, and I have also worked to learn "on my own" how to use various tools in my work (e.g., Facebook, Twitter, web pages, blogs, iPad apps, Google Docs, etc.).*
- *I facilitated online opportunities for students (e.g., A+/Credit Recovery, ACCESS, USA Testprep, etc.) and arranged for purchases through High Hopes to assist at-risk students.*
- *I worked with other directors to select programs for benchmark assessments (STAR vs. Global Scholars, etc.).*
- *I am a member of the ALSDE Assessment and Accountability Task Force, in which online assessments (ACT, ACT-Aspire, etc.) were selected for implementation within an aligned assessment framework.*
- *I worked with the system testing coordinator, technology department, schools, and others, to train teachers.*

- *I facilitated and coordinated the first livestreaming opportunity for graduation ceremonies in Madison County Schools.*
- *I helped envision and coordinate a TIMs (Technology Integration Mentors) program and administrator PLU in Madison County Schools.*

Responsibility of the superintendent regarding technology:

- *Review/update system and school plans;*
- *Address maintenance/upgrade/sustainability issues where technology currently exists and listen and collaborate with those at the system and school levels to plan for "next steps" for growth in technology (e.g., weigh pros/cons and educate students, parents, and employees along the way regarding responsible use);*
- *Look at responsible ways technology can help us be more efficient at the school and system levels.*

Co-Curricular Activities

I believe that co-curricular activities are very important in reaching the goal of providing a variety of opportunities so all students can "find their niche," so to speak, to get involved outside of the classroom in activities that are important to them. We must identify and develop the interests, aptitudes, and values of students not only through academics, but also through co-curricular activities. Clubs, fine arts, athletics, and so forth, are all ways students can become and remain engaged in the educational experience.

Fine Arts

The arts provide an important avenue in which students can develop a passion for learning. Many young people discover their talents and interests through the arts and are inspired to pursue careers in artistic fields. An ASCD article (January 2013) entitled "Ten Reasons Arts Education Matters" listed the following benefits of arts education: (1) the arts can increase student engagement; (2) children learn positive habits, behaviors, and attitudes; (3) the arts enhance creativity; (4) students sharpen their critical intellectual skills; (5) the arts teach students methods for learning language skills; (6) the arts help students learn mathematics; (7) the arts expand on and enrich learning in other subjects; (8) aesthetic learning is its own reward; (9) students practice teamwork; and (10) arts education is just the beginning.

Athletics

Athletics programs are also very important. In addition to helping develop necessary skills, athletic programs can provide each participant with experiences that are positive and memorable and will help develop capacity for commitment to a cause, acceptance of responsibility, and loyalty toward a chosen endeavor. Through participation in athletics, students can benefit from the development of physical fitness, leadership, teamwork, social skills, self-discipline, and character. Decision-making skills, good citizenship, sportsmanship, and individual maturity should also result from athletic participation. These characteristics assist in the development of individual and team attitudes that are beneficial for a successful season, as well as for students' futures. Athletics programs provide opportunities for schools to engage students, parents, and community members in activities that can be a source of great pride not only for the students/employees in a school, but also for the system, community, and so forth. I believe the following guidelines provide solid parameters for athletics programs from middle school through varsity athletics:

- *At the middle school, freshman, and junior varsity levels, emphasis is on skill development and participation, as well as team success. However, the school does not adhere to an "all players get equal playing time" policy even at these levels. At the varsity level, team success and performance become more primary objectives.*
- *Especially at the middle school level, coaches must understand the following:*

  -Students have varying levels of ability, and coaches need to present a developmentally appropriate program for student-athletes.
  -Positive encouragement is the strongest tool for learning.
  -Coaches should provide a safe environment for students to experiment and grow.
  -Activities should be meaningful and fun.
  -Fundamentals and practice are the building blocks for a successful athlete.
  -Every team member's responsibility is to encourage other teammates.
  -Today's superstar could be tomorrow's bench warmer, and vice versa.

"Sportsmanship in athletics as well as in everyday life is more important than the rewards of winning. For long after the joys of winning have faded, or the sting of defeat is past, it is how we responded to the outcome of the game that people remember. Knowing how to handle victory or

defeat says a lot about the person we are, or the person we are becoming." (Calvin Turnipseed)

Career and Technical Education

Career and Technical Education has changed dramatically over the past few years. CTE opportunities are no longer "just for kids who are not going to college"—to the contrary, it is very much for those students. CTE programs provide opportunities for hands-on learning, opportunities to leave high school with credentials/certifications in various areas, and so forth. Of the five areas in which students can demonstrate "college- and career-readiness" (qualifying score on an AP/IB exam, successful completion of a dual enrollment course, benchmark score on ACT, benchmark on WorkKeys, and/or industry-certified credential), three involve CTE. This speaks to the importance of Career and Technical Education today.

Special Education, etc.

With regard to special needs students, including gifted/talented and English-language learner students, I would work very closely with the special education director and others to make sure we are meeting the needs of our students with special needs and that we are taking advantage of every opportunity for our other students to interact with them and work together so everyone can learn from each other. I truly believe that every student deserves to have an "individualized education plan" to meet his or her unique needs.

Plan 2020

The state board of education adopted the Superintendent's Plan 2020 to set educational goals across all systems with the following vision: Every Child a Graduate—Every Graduate Prepared for College/Work/Adulthood in the 21st Century. The four areas of focus within the plan are as follows:

- *Learners*
- *Professionals*
- *Schools/Systems*
- *Support Systems*

Each area includes specific objectives, strategies, and indicators/targets that are important in achieving goals. Absolutes during the transition are very important:

- *Teach to the standards for each of the required subjects (Alabama College- and Career-Ready Standards—Courses of Study);*
- *Through a clearly articulated and locally aligned K–12 curriculum (Sample curricula found on ALEX and Alabama Insight);*
- *Supported by aligned resources, support, and professional development (sample lesson plans and supporting resources found on ALEX, differentiated support through ALSDE regional support teams and ALSDE initiatives, etc.);*
- *Monitored regularly through formative, interim/benchmark assessments to inform the effectiveness of instruction and continued learning needs of individuals and groups of students (GlobalScholar, QualityCore benchmarks, and other locally determined assessments);*
- *With the goal that each student graduates from high school with the knowledge and skills to succeed in post–high school education and the workforce without the need for remediation, as evidenced by multiple measures achieved through multiple pathways to meet the graduation requirements set for students in Alabama (Alabama High School Graduation Requirements/Diploma).*

All of this fits together through a CIP (continuous improvement plan), formative assessments, professional learning, Educate/LEAD AL, accountability, and "College- and Career-Ready Students." Individual capacity (individuals get better) and collective capacity (groups get better) are critical in this process. "The big collective capacity and the one that ultimately counts is when they get better conjointly—collective, collaborative capacity" (Michael Fullen).

Accountability

I would work to instill a culture of personal accountability for student performance across the school system by doing the following:

- *Establish and maintain clear expectations (and explain how these expectations relate to the overall mission of the system);*
- *Define individual responsibilities (and how these responsibilities are critically important to the achievement of goals);*
- *Monitor progress on a regular basis (using formative and summative data);*
- *Celebrate and recognize achievements and directly address areas of concern;*
- *Model personal accountability (encouraging a teamwork approach, but with a "the buck stops here" attitude).*

My goal would be to create and maintain a culture of continuous improvement, monitoring data and listening to stakeholders and making changes when needed.

Ninety-Day Plan of Action

If I am selected as superintendent, the following would be some of my priorities during the first ninety days:

- *Make sure I am prepared before January 1st to have a smooth and seamless transition of leadership for the system;*
- *Meet individually with board members, system/school administrators, key leaders in the community, and so forth, to begin developing relationships and identify common themes that will likely emerge from those conversations to help guide "next steps";*
- *Visit all schools on an ongoing basis and attend as many school/community activities as possible;*
- *Move to Scottsboro, visit churches, get settled/involved in the community.*

My Commitment to You

If selected for this very important position, I will work very hard as a part of a team to keep the system moving forward on the path of continuous improvement. I will work hard to establish relationships with all stakeholders based on trust, candor, and respect. I will not compromise my integrity or that of this system, and I will remember that I am a humble servant who has been entrusted with a tremendous responsibility that will be taken very seriously. I will remember that we are here for the students and will try to keep everyone focused in every situation on what is best for our students. And I will pray daily for wisdom, guidance, and favor, not only for myself, but for all of us as we have been entrusted with a most precious gift, the young people of this community.

I am honored to be one of the finalists for this position, and I will be honored if I am selected to serve as superintendent of Scottsboro City Schools. Thank you for the opportunity to interview for this job!

Appendix E: A Note About Childhaven

She is sixteen years old, and says, "It's the last week of the month. I can call my Mom!" I looked a little puzzled, so she explains that her mom used her monthly check to buy booze at the first of the month, but it would run out the third week. During the last week of the month, she would be sober enough to have an understandable conversation. She is just one of the nearly 175 individuals touched by Childhaven each day.

Childhaven is a Christian children's home. We serve abused, neglected, and needy children on our Cullman, Alabama, campus, and serve foster children and their families in a family reunification/preservation ministry. This place has a rich history, with the original home's dedication taking place on Mother's Day weekend in 1910! Through the decades this has always been a place where marginalized children find a new beginning, and find hope for a better future. Literally thousands of lives have been changed.

Childhaven has always sought to find ways to best benefit and impact the children and families we serve. In the early 1900s, children were housed in barracks with a matron for every thirty or more children. Most of these children are no longer with us, but those who remain tell us the children truly "ran the place"! Childhaven was among the earliest to develop group homes, using a live-in house parent model to serve smaller groups of children in a homelike setting. We remain dedicated to providing a Christian homelike setting for each child to live in. We were among the first to develop specialized, transitional, and independent living programs, to better prepare older youth for life beyond foster care.

When a pilot program was announced to serve entire families, in an effort to prevent parents losing children into foster care, or to successfully bring those children home again (reunification), Childhaven was chosen to be a part of that pilot. That program is no longer a pilot, and is part of our ministry today. We have seen other programs develop as well. For example, for many years we offered GED classes on campus for our older youth, and provided tutoring and educational support for all of our school-aged children. Since our beginning, we have encouraged each child to go on to college or university, and provide the support to make that possible. Our commitment is to be "out front," leading the way in finding more effective ways to serve our marginalized families, children, and youth.

As most of us realize, today's child lives in a rapidly changing and somewhat scary world. Family structures are in flux, technology is changing how we interact with one another and the world, and information is growing rapidly and is instantly available! Even youth from the best of homes are often struggling to find their footing. Those who are part of the Childhaven "family" are arriving with great needs—emotional, spiritual, educational, and social. *Never has the task of leadership been more important!*

That's why I am so excited about this book. Dr. Jan Harris has woven an easy to read story that presents seven critical leadership principles. Each principle is based upon the Old Testament writings of King Solomon from the book of Proverbs. King Solomon is widely seen as the wisest man of all time. Solomon knew how to assess a knotty and difficult situation. He found ways to gather all the information he needed, and then he executed a path forward in a manner that was understood and respected, and that worked! This volume highlights how the biblical wisdom of Solomon can impact the leadership practices in the education arena. Though this book is focused on educational leadership, these principles are timeless. They apply to all in leadership positions, whatever their profession may be.

All the proceeds from each book will benefit the work of Childhaven. These funds will provide for the care of our abused, neglected, and impoverished children. As you read, find encouragement in knowing that your purchase is making a difference in their lives.

"Jill" truly gave us a "run for her money!" We saw one another recently, and she immediately came across the room to thank us for "not giving up on her." Today she has a university degree (engineering), is a leader in her job, happily married with one child, and active in her church, and has recently found the courage to begin sharing her life story. And I could share many more stories like hers. I suspect that each of you can also share similar stories. Never has your leadership been more important. Now, read and enjoy. Use these biblical principles to enhance your role as a leader!

Dr. Jim Wright
Executive Director, Childhaven, Inc.
www.childhaven.com

Appendix F: Leadership, According to Solomon

WISE LEADERS POSSESS SEVEN QUALITIES:

1. Vision
Where there is no vision, the people perish. Proverbs 29:18

_____

_____

2. Knowledge
Pay attention and listen to the sayings of the wise. Proverbs 22:17

_____

_____

3. Ethics
By justice a king gives a country stability, but those who are greedy for bribes tear it down. Proverbs 29:4

_____

_____

4. Humility
When pride comes, then comes disgrace, but with humility comes wisdom. Proverbs 11:2

_____

_____

5. Self-Control

A fool gives full vent to his anger, but a wise man keeps himself under control. Proverbs 29:11

_____

_____

6. Counsel
Plans fail for lack of counsel, but with many advisors they succeed. Proverbs 15:22

_____

_____

7. Understanding
Be sure you know the condition of your flocks. . . . Proverbs 27:23

_____

_____

Appendix G: Graphic of Crown

References

Covey, S. R. 1989. *The Seven Habits of Highly Effective People.* New York: Simon & Schuster.

DuFour, R., and R. Marzano. 2011. *Leaders of Learning: How District, School, and Classroom Leaders Improve Student Achievement.* Bloomington, IN: Solution Tree.

Ehrich, L. C., B. Hansford, and L. Tennent. 2004. "Formal Mentoring Programs in Education and Other Professions: A Review of the Literature." *Educational Administration Quarterly,* 40(4): 518–40.

Hoerr, T. R. 2005. *The Art of Leadership.* Alexandria, VA: Association for Supervision and Curriculum Development.

Kouzes, J. M., and B. Z. Posner. 2003. *Encouraging the Heart: A Leader's Guide to Rewarding and Recognizing Others.* San Francisco: Jossey-Bass.

Kram, K. E. 1985. *Mentoring at Work: Developmental Relationships in Organizational Life.* Lanham, MD: University Press of America.

Lankau, M. J., and T. A. Scandura. 2007. "Mentoring as a Forum for Personal Learning." In *The Handbook of Mentoring at Work: Theory, Research, and Practice,* edited by B. R. Ragins and K. E. Kram, 95–122. Thousand Oaks, CA: Sage Publications.

Lencioni, P. 2002. *The Five Dysfunctions of a Team.* San Francisco: Jossey-Bass.

Levinson, D., D. Darrow, M. Levinson, E. Klein, and B. McKee. 1978. *The Seasons of a Man's Life.* New York: Knopf.

Mendels, P. 2012. "The Effective Principal." *Journal of Staff Development,* 33(1): 54–58.

National Policy Board for Educational Administration. 2015. *Professional Standards for Educational Leaders 2015.* Reston, VA: Author.

Ragins, B. R., and K. E. Kram, eds. 2007. *The Handbook of Mentoring at Work: Theory, Research, and Practice.* Thousand Oaks, CA: Sage Publications.

Ramaswami, G., and G. F. Dreher. 2010. "Mentoring Relationships in India: A Qualitative Exploratory Study." *Human Resource Management,* 49(3): 501–30.

Reeves, D. B. 2006. *The Learning Leader: How to Focus School Improvement for Better Results.* Alexandria, VA: Association for Supervision and Curriculum Development.

Shaw, G. B. 1903. *Man and Superman.* Cambridge, MA: The University Press.

Van Biema, D. 2007. "The Case for Teaching the Bible." *Time,* April 2, 40–46.

Whiston, W. 1998. *Josephus, The Complete Works.* Nashville: Thomas Nelson, Inc.

Contributors

SENATOR PAUL BUSSMAN

Senator Paul Bussman is currently serving his second term in the Alabama Senate. Senator Bussman attended Troy State University, where he was a four-year letterman and received his bachelor of science degree. He then attended the University of Alabama, School of Dentistry, where he received his doctor of dental medicine degree. Senator Bussman has been a general dentist in Cullman since 1983. He has held many offices, including five national appointments in the Academy of General Dentistry.

Paul has devoted countless volunteer hours to committees and organizations such as the Good Samaritan Health Clinic, Habitat for Humanity, and Volunteers in Public Schools. His efforts have improved the quality of life of many Cullman residents. Paul and his wife, Holly, have been married for more than seventeen years. Their children, Noah, 13, and Kendall, 7, live at home in Cullman, while their children Phillip and Melissa live and work in Alabama.

DR. BARRY CARROLL

After thirty years in public education in Alabama, Dr. Barry Carroll retired as superintendent of education to join Promethean. Dr. Carroll worked for Promethean in Atlanta for three years prior to accepting a vice president position with Curriculum Advantage in Atlanta. Dr. Carroll's career in education consisted of serving as a teacher, assistant principal, and principal in Tuscaloosa, Alabama. He served as a middle school principal in Huntsville, Alabama, and later served as the director of secondary education and professional development. In 2001, Dr. Carroll became the superintendent of education for the Limestone County Schools in Athens, Alabama, where he served for ten years. In 2005, the Alabama School Communicators Association named him Superintendent of the Year.

Dr. Carroll earned his bachelor of education degree from Alabama A&M University in Huntsville, Alabama; two master of arts degrees from the University of Alabama in Tuscaloosa; and his doctor of education degree in administration and educational leadership from the University of Alabama.

MR. BILLY COLEMAN

Billy Coleman started his career in Alexander City, Alabama, as a speech teacher and coach. He later taught and coached at three high schools in Alabama. He served as principal of West Point High School and Superintendent of the Cullman County School System in Alabama.

He has been an inspirational speaker for over forty years, speaking with teacher and student groups, civic organizations, business groups, and churches. Billy has written two inspirational books: *Called to Live* and *He Always Holds up the Heavy End*. Billy and his wife Shireen presently live in Alexander City, Alabama, where they lead a citywide leadership group called Legacy Builders and work with college students at Central Alabama Community College. They have been married for thirty-eight years, and have two sons and four grandchildren.

DR. EARL FRANKS

L. Earl Franks is the executive director of the National Association of Elementary School Principals. Before assuming this post, Dr. Franks served as the executive director of the Council for Leaders in Alabama Schools since 2008. Prior to joining CLAS in this position, he served as a leader on the CLAS board of directors and the Alabama Association of Secondary School Principals board of directors. He has twenty-two years of experience in public education, working with all grades. Dr. Franks served as a principal from 1999 until 2008 at Luverne School (Alabama), a PreK–12 school serving over one thousand students. Prior to his selection as principal, Earl was an award-winning band director for thirteen years.

Dr. Franks is a Multiple Paul Harris Fellow with Major Donor distinction of Rotary International and has received leadership awards from the Alabama Music Educators Association and Troy University Music Department, as well as the prestigious Certified Association Executive (CAE) credential from the CAE Commission of ASAE, the Center for Association Leadership. Dr. Franks received his bachelor of music education, master of science in education, and educational specialist degrees from Troy University. He received his doctorate in educational leadership from Samford University in Birmingham, Alabama. Dr. Franks is married to Carol Franks, an associate professor of music at Troy University.

MS. GAIL MORGAN

Gail Morgan has served as professional development coordinator for the Council for Leaders in Alabama Schools (CLAS) since March 2011. Prior to this, she was the professional development assistant Coordinator for two years. A diverse educational career in public, private, and parochial schools in Alabama and Louisiana has afforded many unique opportunities. She was an assistant principal at Luverne School in Crenshaw County, Alabama, a PreK–12 school with over one thousand students. During her twenty-plus years in education she has taught all grade levels, PreK through grade 12.

Numerous trainings on diverse topics have been presented by Gail at the local and state level. Gail also has been privileged to share nationally and internationally through the National Association of Elementary School Principals (NAESP), American Association of School Personnel Administrators (AASPA) and Learning Forward. Gail and her husband, Jimmy, reside in Montgomery, Alabama. They have two adult sons and a daughter-in-law.

JEREMY ODEN

Jeremy H. Oden was appointed to the Place 1 vacancy on the Alabama Public Service Commission (PSC) in 2012, and elected to a full term in 2014. Previously, Oden was elected as a member of the Alabama House of Representatives. He was first elected to the State House in 1998 and represented District 11 (Cullman, Blount, and Morgan Counties) until his appointment to the PSC.

Before his appointment, Oden worked in the financial industry as branch manager and vice president for Eva Bank in Cullman, Alabama. He was also a small business owner, primarily involved in the construction industry. Oden is a proud Christian and an ordained minister. He holds a bachelor's degree from Asbury University and completed two years of post-graduate seminary studies.

DR. LINDA SEARBY

Dr. Linda Searby, PhD, is an associate clinical professor of educational leadership at the University of Florida. She previously served as a mentoring researcher and associate professor at Auburn University in Auburn, Alabama. She teaches courses in personal and professional development, action

research, and supervision of personnel, as well as mentoring in the educational leadership master's program, EdS, and PhD programs. She is the senior
coeditor of the *International Journal of Mentoring and Coaching in Education*, and serves on the executive board of the International Mentoring Association.

Dr. Searby coauthored the book *Best Practices in Mentoring for Teacher
and Leader Development* in 2016, and has over twenty journal publications
in her areas of research, which focus on development of a mentoring mindset
in protégés, and on assistant principals and their mentoring needs as leaders.

DR. SANDRA SPIVEY

Dr. Sandra Spivey is from Scottsboro, Alabama. At Auburn University, she
completed her bachelor of science in mathematics and English secondary
education and her master's in mathematics education. She later completed
her masters certification in educational administration and her education specialist degree in educational leadership at Auburn University Montgomery,
then went on to complete her doctorate in educational leadership at Auburn
University in 2004. Dr. Spivey served as a high school math teacher, cheerleading coach, and sponsor of various clubs and programs. She later served
as a high school assistant principal as well as a middle school and high
school principal. She also served as the director of human resources for
Hoover City Schools.

In 2007, she accepted the position of Director of Secondary Education for
Madison County Schools. She remained there for seven years before accept-
ing a position with the Alabama State Department of Education as a Regional
Support Coordinator. She is now back home in Scottsboro, where she has
served as the Superintendent of the Scottsboro City School System since
January of 2015.

About the Author

Dr. Jan Irons Harris

Dr. Jan Irons Harris, a lifelong educator whose mission is to teach others a better way of life through education and love and by example, using her gifts of teaching and leading, was born in Florence, Alabama. She earned her bachelor's and master's degrees in math and education from the University of North Alabama and the University of South Carolina, respectively. She received her doctorate in school administration from Peabody College of Vanderbilt University, where she received the Wheeler Prize for Outstanding Academic Achievement in Doctoral Studies. Jan has served as a secondary math teacher, assistant principal, middle and high school principal, and superintendent. Currently, she serves as superintendent of Dade County Schools in Trenton, Georgia.

In 2001, Jan was named Alabama PTA High School Principal of the Year, and Alumnus of the Year at the University of North Alabama. Dr. Harris was selected as Alabama District VIII Superintendent of the Year in 2009. In 2010, she was selected as one of ten Tech-Savvy Superintendents in the nation by eSchool news. She was named the 2010 Cullman Times Distinguished Citizen of the Year, and the Women of Distinction Outstanding Educator by the North-Central Alabama Girl Scouts. In 2012, she received the Heart of An Eagle Award from the Boy Scouts of America. In 2013, Mayor Max Townson named Jan an Honorary Cullman "Colonel," and Childhaven presented its Dot Causey Distinguished Service Award to Jan and her husband, Wholey.

Jan is an active member of her church and community. She is the author of *The Principal's Office: A Primer for Balanced Leadership* (Rowman and Littlefield Education Publishers, 2008).

Leadership, According to Solomon